Urban North-

Dialects of English

Volumes available in the series:
Robert McColl Millar, *Northern and Insular Scots*
David Deterding, *Singapore English*
Jennifer Hay, Margaret Maclagan and Elizabeth Gordon, *New Zealand English*
Pingali Sailaja, *Indian English*
Karen P. Corrigan, *Irish English, volume 1 – Northern Ireland*
Jane Setter, Cathy S. P. Wong and Brian H. S. Chan, *Hong Kong English*
Joan Beal, Lourdes Burbano-Elizondo and Carmen Llamas, *Urban North-Eastern English: Tyneside to Teesside*

Visit the Dialects of English website at www.euppublishing.com/series/DIOE

Urban North-Eastern English: Tyneside to Teesside

Joan C. Beal, Lourdes Burbano-Elizondo and Carmen Llamas

EDINBURGH
University Press

© Joan C. Beal, Lourdes Burbano-Elizondo and Carmen Llamas, 2012

Edinburgh University Press Ltd
22 George Square, Edinburgh EH8 9LF

www.euppublishing.com

Typeset in 10.5/12 Janson
by Servis Filmsetting Ltd, Stockport, Cheshire, and
printed and bound in Great Britain by
CPI Group (UK) Ltd, Croydon, CR0 4YY

A CIP record for this book is available from the British Library

ISBN 978 0 7486 3929 8 (hardback)
ISBN 978 0 7486 4152 9 (paperback)
ISBN 978 0 7486 6445 0 (webready PDF)
ISBN 978 0 7486 6447 4 (ePub)
ISBN 978 0 7486 6446 7 (Amazon ebook)

The right of Joan C. Beal, Lourdes Burbano-Elizondo and Carmen Llamas
to be identified as authors of this work
has been asserted in accordance with
the Copyright, Designs and Patents Act 1988.

Contents

List of figures and tables

Acknowledgements

We are all extremely grateful to the members of the advisory board of the Dialects of English series and to the anonymous referees for their helpful comments on the proposal for this volume. We are especially grateful to April McMahon for her suggestions for improvements of initial drafts and to Vicki Donald for her help and patience. Thanks to friends and colleagues for their encouragement and willingness to read our drafts, listen to our ideas and contribute their own. Special mention is due to Chris Montgomery, Paul Foulkes, Peter French, Lisa Roberts, Paula Sochanik and Dominic Watt. Thanks to the Research Development Fund of Edge Hill University for granting Lourdes research leave and to Damien for his support and proof-reading. Last but not least, thanks to all the canny lads and lasses from Tyne to Tees who so willingly gave their time, voices and opinions to make this possible.

Map of locations referred to in this book

1 History, geography, demography and culture

1.1 Introduction

The North-East region of England stretches from the Scottish border in the north to the southern banks of the River Tees in the south and is delimited to the west by the Pennines and the county boundaries of Northumberland and Durham with Cumbria. Since this volume deals with urban varieties of North-Eastern English, we will be concentrating on the more densely populated southern part of the region, between the rivers Tyne and Tees, and mostly on the conurbations of Newcastle and Gateshead on the Tyne, Sunderland on the Wear and Middlesbrough on the Tees. This chapter is intended to introduce readers to the region, stressing both the factors which unite these three urban centres and those which distinguish them from each other.

1.2 Geography

1.2.1 The North-East

The geography of this region is dominated by the Pennines to the west, the North Sea coast to the east and the three major rivers, the Tyne, Wear and Tees. It is the most northerly region of England, stretching as it does to the border town of Berwick-upon-Tweed, and Newcastle is the most northerly city in England. Despite the fact that the region is served by two major road transport links to the south, the A1/M1 and the A19, by the East Coast rail line and by two international airports, Newcastle and Durham Tees Valley, this remoteness from the capital has led to a perception of the region being a place apart from the rest of England, as described by the Teesside-born author Harry Pearson:

> In the North-East, England, or rather the notion of England, seems a long way off. The North-East is at the far corner of the country, but it is separated

by more than miles. There is the wilderness of the Pennines to the west, the emptiness of the North Yorkshire moors to the south and to the north the Scottish border. The nearest major city to Newcastle is Edinburgh, and that is in another country. (1994: 136–7)

1.2.2 Newcastle and Tyneside

As we shall see in section 1.3.2, there has been a settlement at the lowest bridging point of the Tyne since Roman times and the 'new' castle which gave the city its name was built by the Normans. Both sets of invaders recognised the strategic importance of this site as the last outpost of their respective domains. Geologically, the most important factor in shaping the identity of the Tyneside conurbation is the presence of large coal deposits: the phrase 'to carry coals to Newcastle' as a proverb, meaning to supply with a commodity already held in excess, is cited in the *Oxford English Dictionary* as early as 1660, but an earlier citation of 'as common as coales from Newcastle' in 1606 proves that this association goes back further. Newcastle is on the north bank of the Tyne and was formerly the principal city in the county of Northumberland, whereas Gateshead on the south bank was part of County Durham, but since the two were brought together in an unsuccessful bid for the European City of Culture in 2008, they have been promoted as a single destination for tourists and business travellers, NewcastleGateshead: 'United by seven bridges across a spectacular riverscape, Newcastle (a city on the north bank of the River Tyne) and Gateshead (a town on the south bank) form a single, diverse and extremely vibrant visitor destination' (http://www. newcastlegateshead.com/site/about-the-area/newcastlegateshead).

The newcastlegateshead.com site covers the coastal resorts of Whitley Bay, Tynemouth and South Shields, which, along with the fishing port of North Shields and the shipbuilding and former colliery town of Wallsend, make up (with Newcastle and Gateshead) the Tyneside conurbation. It also includes Sunderland, which was brought into the new metropolitan county of Tyne and Wear in 1974. As we shall see in section 1.5, the inclusion of Sunderland is locally controversial, given the rivalry between its citizens and those of Newcastle.

1.2.3 Sunderland and Wearside

The City of Sunderland is situated on the mouth of the River Wear, around 15 miles (24km) to the south of Newcastle upon Tyne and just under 30 miles (48km) to the north of the Teesside conurbation. The city has spread on both banks of the river, though the part of Sunderland that lies on the southern bank, where we find the city centre, is the most extensive and populous.

With a population of 280,807 in the 2001 Census,[1] Sunderland is the second largest city in the North-East after Newcastle. It is one of the many boroughs/areas in the region that were affected by the reorganisation of county boundaries of 1974. Until then, Sunderland had been part of County Durham, an area whose northern boundary was marked by the River Tyne, as mentioned in the previous section. However, with the reconfiguration of regional boundaries, Sunderland became part of the new metropolitan county of Tyne and Wear. At the same time, other mining towns/districts, such as Washington, Houghton-le-Spring, Hetton-le-Hole and Fence Houses, which until then had been part of County Durham, too were re-aligned as part of the metropolitan borough of the City of Sunderland.

Arguably, these political changes impacted on the local social identity not only of Sunderland people, who now were part of a new metropolitan county together with Newcastle upon Tyne, but also of the inhabitants of Washington, Houghton, Hetton and the neighbouring villages and towns, who were not only part of a new county now but also of the Sunderland borough. Furthermore, the River Tyne, which, historically, had served as a political boundary between County Durham and Northumberland, ceased to be such a political divide and peoples to the north and south of this landmark were administratively brought together by the new political boundaries.

1.2.4 Middlesbrough and Teesside

Middlesbrough, as we will see in section 1.3.4, owes its 'birth' in the nineteenth century and its very existence as an urban centre to its geographical position along the River Tees. Middlesbrough lies closer to the mouth of the river than Stockton-on-Tees (the site of the railway line along which the first ever steam-powered passenger train ran in 1825). In order to avoid the navigational hazards of the Tees, an extension was made to the railway line to Middlesbrough to allow for the easier conveyance of coal to the south. This, combined with the discovery of iron ore in the nearby Cleveland Hills, meant that the geographical position of Middlesbrough was central to its expansion and development as the largest urban centre of the conurbation around the Tees.

The position in relation to the river of the various urban centres which form the Teesside conurbation (Middlesbrough, Stockton-on-Tees, Hartlepool, Thornaby, Billingham, Redcar, Darlington) has also had significance for the political identity of the locations in terms of county boundaries and local administrative areas. The changes in these boundaries in the latter part of the twentieth century have led to shifts in local orientations, as discussed further in section 1.3.3.

1.3 History

1.3.1 The North-East

The North-East was not designated as an official region of England for government purposes until 1994, but the area included in this region has been perceived and treated as a distinct and separate part of England since at least Anglo-Saxon times. For the Romans, the north of England as far as Hadrian's Wall was designated '*Britannia Inferior*', while the uncon-quered territory beyond was '*Britannia Barbara*'. The Wall stretches from Wallsend on the north bank of the Tyne to the Solway Firth on the west coast and runs slightly to the north of the A69 road. This means that most of the urban areas discussed in this volume would have been south of the Wall, with Tyneside on the frontier. After the Romans departed, Anglian tribes from what is now the north of Germany and Denmark settled in the north and east of England, eventually founding Northumbria after the union of Bernicia (north of the Tees) and Deira (between the Tees and the Humber). As the name indicates, this kingdom's southern border was the River Humber and, since it also included territory as far north as the Firth of Forth, it encompassed part of what is today Scotland. From the earliest written records it is evident that the dialect spoken in Northumbria was different from those in other kingdoms, especially the Saxon settlements in the south and west.

Later in the Old English period, Scandinavian settlements were concentrated in the south of the region: if we search the University of Nottingham's *Key to English Place Names* for names including the Scandinavian element *-by* we find none in Northumberland (except possibly Byker), three in county Durham, all in the far south of the county (Aislaby, Killerby and Raby with Keverstone), but eighty-nine in North Yorkshire. As we shall see in section 4.3, words of Scandinavian origin are likewise more numerous in Teesside than in Tyneside or Wearside. In the following sections, we will discuss the distinct historical developments of these three urban areas.

1.3.2 Newcastle and Tyneside

The Romans established three forts on Hadrian's Wall within the area we now call Tyneside: Condercum in what is now the western suburb of Benwell, Segedunum in Wallsend and Pons Aelius, referring to both a bridge over the Tyne and a fort in the centre of the modern city of Newcastle. In Anglo-Saxon times, what had been Pons Aelius developed into a monastic site called Monkchester. It was not until William the Conqueror's eldest son, returning from a raid against the Scots, built a castle on the site of the Roman fort that the settlement took on its present name of Newcastle. A medieval walled town grew up around the castle and the quayside became increasingly important as a seaport. Newcastle was granted its own mayor in 1216 and became a county with its own sheriff in 1400. Although Newcastle did not acquire the status of a city until 1882, its strategic importance as a seaport and as a fortress against the Scots made it an important provincial centre from medieval times. Early travellers from the south attest its status and prosperity: Celia Fiennes, travelling in 1698, described Newcastle as 'a noble town tho' in a bottom' (Fiennes 1947: 209) and wrote that 'it most resembles London of any place in England', while Daniel Defoe described it as 'a large and exceeding populous town' with 'a very noble Exchange' and as 'a place of great Trade and Business' (1753: 221, 222, 224). The main source of this prosperity was coal: in 1239, Henry III granted a charter to the townsmen of Newcastle to dig for coal, but the first real expansion of the coal mining industry and the associated transport of coal by sea to London came in the sixteenth century, not long before 'coals to Newcastle' is first cited. By the middle of the eighteenth century, 'the average annual export of coal from the Tyne' had risen 'to 777,000 tons' (Ellis 2001: 5). Apart from coal, other industries important in Newcastle at this time were salt making, glass and shipbuilding. Of the last, Defoe noted that 'they build Ships here to Perfection as to Strength and Firmness and to bear the Sea as the Coal Trade requires' (1753: 225). Shipbuilding was to be a major industry on Tyneside until the second half of the twentieth century, buoyed up by the demand for warships created by the two world wars. The nineteenth century also saw the growth of heavy engineering with companies such as Armstrong's flourishing. Like the shipbuilding industry, engineering was sustained through the first half of the twentieth century by the demand for armaments.

The nineteenth century also saw the expansion of Newcastle as a commercial and retail centre: what was 'arguably the first department store in England' (Lendrum 2001: 37) was opened by Emerson Bainbridge in 1838. This was followed by Fenwick's in 1882, establishing Newcastle as a major regional shopping centre. Natasha Vall informs us that:

In 1927, J. Robinson, Chairman of the Retail Section of the Chamber of Commerce, called for greater appreciation of the 'service' rendered to the city by its many shopkeepers, and particularly from the regional railway companies indebted to the retailers for encouraging 'people to travel in their 1000s to Newcastle, where the life of the city is largely centred in its shops'. (Vall 2001: 61)

Vall presents a picture of early twentieth-century Newcastle which is a counterbalance to the prevailing stereotype of poverty and deprivation. She relates that in 1936 (the same year as the Jarrow March, in which 200 unemployed shipyard workers walked to London in protest), the *Retail Supplement of the Newcastle and Gateshead Chamber of Commerce* 'introduced an anonymous female columnist known as "The Lady Onlooker" to provide a commentary on the city's retailing trends' (2001: 62–3). When heavy industry declined in the mid-twentieth century, the redevelopment of the city centre concentrated on retail, thus sustaining the city's position as a regional centre. Although the opening of the Gateshead Metro Centre in 1986 (still claiming to be the largest shopping and leisure centre in Europe) was thought to provide a potential threat to the retail outlets in Newcastle city centre, it has further consolidated Tyneside as the major regional hub for shopping and leisure.

The most recent regeneration of the Newcastle and Gateshead quaysides has enhanced the city's reputation as a leisure destination, both as a 'party city' centred around the bars and clubs of the Bigg Market and Quayside and as a cultural hub including the Baltic art gallery and the Sage concert hall. The expansion of higher education in Newcastle (the city has a student population of 42,000) has provided a major source of employment, as well as customers for the 'party city'.

1.3.3 Sunderland and Wearside

Although, as indicated in section 1.2.3, the City of Sunderland straddles both the northern and southern banks of the River Wear (but mainly the southern bank), we find the origins of this city in the monastic settlements that developed on the northern bank of the Wear in the second half of the seventh century: this area was, and still is, known as Monkwearmouth. Here, at a time when Roman missionaries were trying to convert Britain to Christianity, Benedict Biscop, a Northumbrian nobleman, founded a monastery at Wearmouth, St Peter's, in an area of land that the Northumbrian king, Egfrith, granted him for this purpose. This monastery was to become a notable centre for culture, learning and religious life in Anglo-Saxon times. Furthermore, St Peter's was the monastery where the Venerable Bede (who is believed to have been born locally) started his monastic life before moving to the monastery founded by Biscop a few years later in Jarrow, by the River Tyne. All monastic life in the North-East, including that at Monkwearmouth, was destroyed in the ninth century as a result of the Viking raids. However, it would later be re-established during the Norman settlement and the church of St Peter's would become part of the Bishopric of Durham.

The port of Wearmouth on the southern bank of the Wear (what today is Sunderland) is thought to have become a borough in 1180, when a charter was awarded that 'granted the same customs to its citizens as those enjoyed by the burgesses of the royal borough of Newcastle upon Tyne' (Dodds 2001: 23). It was around this time that the name 'Sunderland' for what was then the port of Wearmouth began to be used, meaning 'separate land' (land asunder) from the Monkwearmouth community which lived north of the River Wear. Thus, at the time, it was Sunderland that was part of Monkwearmouth and not vice versa (Dodds 2001: 28).

In medieval times, Sunderland and its environs were still economically agriculturally based, even though, from the end of the fourteenth century, coal was being mined and shipped to various destinations. Nevertheless, Sunderland's coal output was dwarfed by that of Tyneside, so Wearside (Sunderland) consequently remained a place of little relevance within the Diocese of Durham relative to its more powerful neighbour.

Sunderland's status improved in the late sixteenth century with the emergence of the salt industry, which used coal from local mines to fuel the furnaces. However, only lower quality/coarse coal was used for salt production, with the higher quality coal exported along with the salt. The development of this new industry created a demand for a large workforce not only in the salt furnaces but also on the Sunderland quays for the loading and shipping of both goods. Ultimately, this provided a notable impetus to the local economy to the point that, in H. L. Robson's words, '[b]y 1600 the port had come to life . . . the commercial town of Sunderland had started its career' (in Dodds 2001: 41). In the course of the seventeenth century, the amount of coal exported from Wearside grew very rapidly and, as a result, Tyneside lost the monopoly in this export. Furthermore, although the amount of coal did not rival that leaving the Tyneside docks, some sources suggest that coal merchants in Tyneside were not happy with this development (Dodds 2001: 42).

Wearside developed as a significant industrial centre over the seventeenth and eighteenth centuries, with glass making, lime and pottery production flourishing. However, it was the development of shipbuilding in the late seventeenth century that transformed the city, so much so that, in the mid-nineteenth century, there were seventy-six shipyards on the Wear. By the mid-twentieth century, more than 20 per cent of Sunderland men worked in either shipbuilding or one of its feeder industries. The twentieth century brought both the zenith and the nadir in the fortunes of shipbuilding on Wearside: from a peak during the Second World War and its immediate aftermath, when ships were in great demand, to the closure of the last shipyard in 1988. A further point to note about shipbuilding on Wearside is that it was not always the preserve of men: during the Second World War, women were employed in the yards in order to make up for the loss of men enlisting in the armed forces.

Shipbuilding was not the only large employer of Wearsiders in the mid-twentieth century: the coal mining industry employed a further 20 per cent of the workforce. Together, these two industries, with their close-knit networks and communities, and which had evolved over centuries on Wearside, had become interwoven in the local identity and what it meant to be a Wearsider. Tragically for the region, coal mining and shipbuilding were to suffer a similar (and almost coterminous) decline, with the last colliery closing in 1993. Clearly, the loss of one such industry would be hard for a region to endure, but the loss of two such industries, that together employed about 40 per cent of the workforce, had devastating social and economic consequences, with soaring unemployment.

Wearside's story in the twentieth century is not all bad, however: female employment has been constantly on the rise since the 1950s and about 50 per cent of the workforce is now female; also, new industries such as car manufacturing have moved in, and Sunderland people have also sought jobs further afield in places like Newcastle (Coombes 2005; Dodds 2001: 145–6). That said, the point to note from all this is that, while Sunderland is recovering, the economic devastation caused by the failure of its major industries in the twentieth century has almost certainly made an indelible mark on conceptualisations of local identity.

1.3.4 Middlesbrough and Teesside

As noted earlier, Middlesbrough was the world's first railway town. Prior to the arrival of the railway in 1830, agriculture dominated the economy and society of Middlesbrough, which consisted of only twenty-five inhabitants in 1801 and forty in 1821 (Moorsom 1996) and was very much smaller than the nearby established towns of Stockton and Darlington.

The development of industry based around iron and steel production in the nineteenth century led to Middlesbrough becoming a boom town, with a population of over 91,000 recorded at the beginning of the twentieth century. The discovery of ironstone in the Cleveland Hills in 1850 ensured that within a mere forty years Middlesbrough had become the biggest producer of pig iron in the world (Chase 1995). The tremendous growth in industry led W. E. Gladstone, on his visit to Middlesbrough in October 1862, famously to declare '[t]his remarkable place, the youngest child of England's enterprise . . . is an infant, gentlemen, but it is an infant Hercules' (in Briggs 1996: 1). Throughout the nineteenth century, people flocked to Middlesbrough looking for work, not only from the town's rural hinterland but also from further afield, especially from Durham, Staffordshire, South Wales, Scotland and Ireland. Such was the 'melting pot' community out of which Middlesbrough English developed.

In the first half of the twentieth century Middlesbrough continued to grow, although not at such a rapid rate as it had in the nineteenth century. Expansion of the industrial base continued, with chemical plants and oil refineries becoming operational along the Tees. As the century progressed the heavy industries went into decline, however. In the second half of the century, shipbuilding on the Tees ceased and the docks were closed. In 1993 the Cleveland Iron Plant was closed, bringing to an end the long tradition of iron making which had begun in 1854 (Moorsom 1996: 38). Since the 1980s the population has been declining. Nonetheless, with a current estimated population of 139,200 (Tees Valley Statistics 2010), Middlesbrough is still the most densely populated of the localities around the Tees and it is the centre of gravity of Teesside.

In terms of orientations and political groupings, the conurbation lies at a major county boundary. The River Tees has traditionally stood as a boundary between County Durham to the north and Yorkshire to the south. Middlesbrough, Thornaby and Redcar lie on the south bank of the River Tees and pre-1968 were situated in the North Riding of Yorkshire. Stockton-on-Tees, Billingham and Hartlepool, on the north bank, were traditionally situated in County Durham. Several changes in local government administrative boundaries were made in the latter part of the twentieth century, however. The county borough of Teesside was formed in 1968 bringing the conurbation along the River Tees together. Six years later, in 1974, the county of Cleveland came into existence. As the urban centre of Hartlepool was included in the new administrative area, the county of Cleveland covered a considerably greater area than the county borough of Teesside. In 1996 Middlesbrough local authority came into existence along with Hartlepool, Stockton-on-Tees, and Redcar and Cleveland local authorities, and in 1997 Darlington also became a unitary authority. These shifts in local political boundaries have had an effect on the orientations and larger regional identities of the inhabitants, and recent work by Llamas (2007) has found that these shifting orientations correlate with phonological changes in progress (see further section 2.7.3).

1.4 Culture

1.4.1 The North-East as a culturally salient region

The *Oxford English Dictionary* defines *North East* as 'The north-eastern part of a country or region; *spec.* the area of England north of the River Humber and east of the Pennines'. However, the only citation given to illustrate this specific sense refers to a more restricted geographical area: '1996 *Sunday Tel.* 13 Oct. (Sport section) 4/8 The renaissance of the North East over the past four years, in football terms, left Sunderland and Middlesbrough panting in the slipstream of Newcastle United' (www.oed.com). Green and Pollard note that a search for the term 'North East' in the archive of *The Times* shows that it is used with reference to this area as a distinct entity from the 1840s (2007: 19). They also assert that 'the perception of the North-east as a region determined by landscape is deeply entrenched and needs no elaboration' (2007: 11). On the other hand, Robert Colls describes the North-East as 'someone else's category error which, nonetheless, has lived to find real meaning' (1998: 198). To outsiders, the North-East is perceived as a single, homogeneous entity dominated by Newcastle and the figure of the 'Geordie', but within the region there are distinct identities and local rivalries.

One measure of the cultural salience of the region and of the dominance of Newcastle is the recognition of the local accent by speakers from other parts of England. Chris Montgomery (2006) conducted a perceptual dialectology study in which he asked participants from Carlisle, Hull and Crewe to name the regional accents of English that they recognised and draw on a blank map of England the areas in which they thought these were spoken. 'Geordie' was the second most recognised accent with a recognition rate of 56.7 per cent (closely behind 'Scouse' at 57.8 per cent). When we look at the composite map compiled from all participants' responses, we see that the area in which 'Geordie' is spoken is perceived as covering the whole of the North-East region (Figure 1.1).

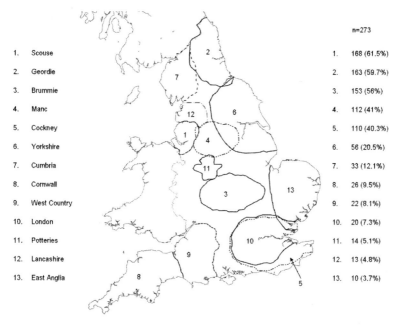

n=273

1.	Scouse		1.	168 (61.5%)
2.	Geordie		2.	163 (59.7%)
3.	Brummie		3.	153 (56%)
4.	Manc		4.	112 (41%)
5.	Cockney		5.	110 (40.3%)
6.	Yorkshire		6.	56 (20.5%)
7.	Cumbria		7.	33 (12.1%)
8.	Cornwall		8.	26 (9.5%)
9.	West Country		9.	22 (8.1%)
10.	London		10.	20 (7.3%)
11.	Potteries		11.	14 (5.1%)
12.	Lancashire		12.	13 (4.8%)
13.	East Anglia		13.	10 (3.7%)

Figure 1.1 Perceptions of dialect areas in England

This contrasts sharply with the perception of Michael Pearce's participants from within the North-East region. Pearce conducted a perceptual study in which participants from locations throughout the region were asked to 'consider fifty one locations across the North East of England' and 'to think about the speech of people in each of these places, assessing the extent of its similarity to or difference from the speech of people in their own hometown' (2009: 166). Pearce found that three distinct perceptual 'sectors' emerged, within which there were seven 'zones'. The 'sectors' were clearly divided into a northern sector centred on Newcastle, a 'central' one around Wearside and much of County Durham, and a 'southern' one incorporating Teesside and Darlington. These sectors correspond very closely to the three varieties described in this volume. Pearce's participants were aware of the tendency for outsiders to perceive the whole of the North-East as a homogeneous region with a single accent ('Geordie') and expressed their feelings of frustration and annoyance when confronted with such perceptions. An example of this is the participant from Sunderland who wrote: 'I am a Wearsider through and through and I think my accent is totally different from the Geordie accent. However, people from outside the North East think we all sound the same and of course we're all Geordies!' (2009: 164).

In the following sections, we will discuss first the cultural and economic dominance of Newcastle and then the nature of the differences and rivalries between Tyneside, Wearside and Teesside.

1.4.2 Newcastle: a regional capital?

We have already seen in section 1.3.2 that Newcastle's economic domination of the North-East goes back several centuries. From being the major seaport and exporter of coal, Newcastle developed into a thriving retail centre in the nineteenth century, with shoppers travelling by rail from other parts of the North-East. More recently, the development of the Eldon Square indoor shopping centre in the city centre and the Metro Centre south of the Tyne, together with the extension of the Tyne and Wear Metro transport system to Sunderland, have all helped Newcastle and the wider Tyneside area retain this dominance even in economically challenging times. The Organisation for Economic Co-operation and Development (OECD) territorial report on Newcastle concludes that it 'exhibits growing integration as a city region and functions as the growth centre of the North East' and notes that 'the economic contribution . . . of Tyneside . . . to the North East economy increased from 33.5% in 1995 to 36.9% in 2003' (OECD 2006: 12).

Natasha Vall discusses the role played by regional broadcasting in establishing Newcastle as the culturally dominant centre of the North-East and 'Geordie' as its voice in the second half of the twentieth century. The music halls of Tyneside had made important contributions to local popular culture in the nineteenth century, with performers such as 'Geordie' Ridley writing and singing in the local dialect (Beal 2000), but the transfer of this local vaudeville tradition to radio in programmes such as *Wot Cheor Geordie* disseminated this further. Vall writes of 'the part played by radio in the process whereby elements of popular culture derived on Tyneside became part of a broader north-eastern cultural characterisation after the Second World War' (2007: 188). The founding of Tyne Tees Television as a regional independent broadcasting company in 1959 further consolidated the perception of this region as a distinct entity. Vall cites a volume celebrating the twentieth anniversary of Tyne Tees TV as follows: '[T]he region stretching from beyond the Tees in the south to well beyond the Tyne in the north, is a region with a culture, a tradition and a way of life entirely of its own' (2007: 193). Vall also notes the importance of 'television dramas and serials such as *The Likely Lads* and *When the Boat Comes In*, that have come to be seen as sustaining north-eastern cultural particularity during the 20th century'

(2007: 191). What is striking to a linguist reviewing these is the diversity of accents in what are perceived as 'Geordie' programmes. James Bolam, who starred in both, was born in Sunderland, while his fellow 'Likely Lad' Rodney Bewes hailed from West Yorkshire, yet neither actor attempted to modify his accent. Since this was the first nationally broadcast TV series to be set on Tyneside, viewers outside the region probably just accepted that the actors were 'northern'. What these programmes did was to bring images and stereotypes of the North-East to a national audience, paving the way for the host of 'Geordie' performers who have contributed to the cultural salience of the region discussed in section 1.4.1.

1.4.3 Local rivalries

In section 1.4.1 we noted the frustration voiced by Pearce's participants from elsewhere in the North-East at being misidentified as 'Geordies'. The same sentiments were expressed by participants from Sunderland and Teesside in the studies by Burbano-Elizondo and Llamas, respectively.

Many of Burbano-Elizondo's (2008) Sunderland participants commented on the fact that dialects from the North-East are generally perceived by the rest of the country as 'Geordie'. Some held the view that this tendency by geographical outsiders to classify Sunderland people as 'Geordies' is generally based on their inability to tell the difference between the various local dialects that exist in the North-East: one respondent claimed that people think that 'everybody from the North-east speaks like "Why aye!"' (MF04);[2] and another, from Washington but studying in Sheffield, explained that people at university tended to call him 'Geordie' because they were not able to distinguish Tyneside English from Sunderland English, yet, Geordies would immediately identify him as a 'Mackem', a term used to refer to people from Sunderland and which derives from the traditional Durham/Sunderland pronunciation of the words *make* and *take*, which is [mak] and [tak] respectively (Beal 1999: 45):[3]

> *I know I get called Geordie sometimes in uni [. . .] But I do know a couple of people from Newcastle or who support Newcastle who class themselves as Geordies so they call me 'Mackem' because they can distinguish it.* (Interview 23 (58:57–59:10))

For many Wearsiders, as was the case for this participant, being misidentified as a Geordie has further negative implications as it is often then presumed that he is a supporter of Newcastle United:

I get . . . annoyed when people . . . call me a Geordie.
<Mm-hm. So that's annoying for you.>
Yes because . . . well I mean although they . . . they pick up at my accent and say oh he's from North-East of England.
<Mm-hm.>
He's from Newcastle.
<Yes.>
It's the first place people think of, which is fair enough.
<Yes it the big place there so.>
Yes but em I . . . I get annoyed because . . .
<You're not a Geordie.>
I associate it with supporting Newcastle United.
(Interview 23 (59:55–60:25))

The cultural and economic dominance of Newcastle is clearly resented by those who perceive themselves as having distinct local identities within the wider North-East region. This was expressed clearly by many of Burbano-Elizondo's (2008) informants when they were asked for their opinions about their region. Although Sunderland was granted city status in 1992 and this considerably boosted pride in the city (Beal 2000: 369), some of the Sunderland participants felt that their city is the less favoured one and that more money is invested in Newcastle, which, in their view, receives all the latest improvements. The following two statements and the extract from one of the interviews indicate the views of three male informants vis-à-vis Newcastle, and reflect negative feelings towards this neighbouring city:

Newcastle is more cosmopolitan and seems to get more business opportunities than Sunderland. Sunderland is clearly the poorer relative. (MM14 – IdQ: qu. 12)

[Newcastle] historically is more important than Sunderland. It has a bigger and better city centre. It [is] seen as the capital of the north. Newcastle is more fashionable than Sunderland, we seem to be the second best on everything including football. (OM07 – IdQ: qu. 12 – aged fifty-one)

But unfortunately the majority of people outside of the North-east, particularly in the south, they don't think there's anything more in the North-east than Newcastle.
<Yeah, yeah that's right.>
<Mm-hm. That true.>
And that's down to f– that's probably down to the fact that Newcastle manages to get everything from the south,
<Uh-huh.>
like, government allocated money to Newcastle.

<Yeah.>
Which is another reason for hating them.
(Interview 15, part 2 (15:42–16:01))

As the citation from the *OED* given in section 1.1.1 implies, the rivalry between Wearside/Teesside and Newcastle is expressed most vehemently with respect to football. Unlike many other English cities – such as Birmingham, Liverpool and Manchester – Newcastle, Sunderland and Middlesbrough each have only one professional football ('soccer') team. This means that rivalry is based not on sectarian or historical occupational grounds as in some cities, but on local allegiance. The 'derby' match is an important institution in British sport, pitting teams against their closest local rivals and accompanied by much 'hype' in the media. Typical derby matches are Liverpool FC vs Everton, Manchester United vs Manchester City and, perhaps most notoriously, the sectarian 'Old Firm' derby between the traditionally Roman Catholic Glasgow Celtic and the traditionally Protestant Glasgow Rangers. Llamas found that, when asked what they considered the local derby match to be, older Teessiders replied that this would be Middlesbrough FC vs Leeds United, while younger Teessiders perceived it to be the fixture against Newcastle United and/or Sunderland. This correlated with a tendency for the older participants to identify with Yorkshire and the younger ones with the North-East region. To football supporters from Tyneside or Wearside, the most important derby match is that between Sunderland and Newcastle United. Indeed, the term *Mackem* as a nickname for a citizen of Sunderland, has its first citation in the *OED* from a Newcastle United fanzine, although the phrase *mak 'em and tak 'em*, supposedly alluding to the shipbuilding trade in Sunderland, has a longer pedigree.

Although football is the main focus of local rivalry within the North-East today, the evidence available seems to suggest that in the case of Wearside the roots of this rivalry may go as far back as the English Civil War, in the mid-seventeenth century. Other factors that have supposedly contributed to the tensions include trade and heavy industry (shipbuilding and coal mining, for example, are seen as strong symbols of Sunderland for those within and outside the community) (Dodds 2001; House 1969: 172) and the economic dominance of Newcastle. The coal trade, for example, may have been the provoker of rivalries between Tyneside and Wearside in the eighteenth century. In connection with this, Dodds (2001: 59) explains that the establishment of the River Wear Commission by an Act of Parliament to improve and maintain the harbour in the River Wear in 1717 was not welcome in Newcastle as this would favour the rise of Sunderland's coal trade even further and some decline in the amount of coal Tyneside exported. Within a few years of this commission being formed, in 1725, following a visit to Newcastle, the Earl of Oxford noted that:

> They [the persons involved in the coal trade] seem at present a little jealous of Sunderland which has of late shared with it pretty considerably in this trade and as I am told is likely to gain more and more upon it every day. (Dodds 2001: 59–60)

In her exploration of how the Sunderland community is created and imagined by its constituent members, Burbano-Elizondo (2008) found that for many, especially among those in the older generations, the rivalry has existed for a long time now, and they often pointed to the industrial past of the two cities (for example, the rivalry between shipbuilders on the Tyne and the Wear) and a desire by their respective populations to be better than the other as the reason that fostered that rivalry in the past. Others referred to the Civil War (in 1642) when Newcastle sided with Charles I and Sunderland with Cromwell's parliamentarians (Dodds 2001: 46). All this is expressed in the following statements about the Geordie–Mackem rivalry (Burbano-Elizondo 2008):

> *[The rivalry was] Brought into focus by football rivalry. Some industrial apartheid. Civil War rivalry, possibly started with rivalry over the coal trade in the Middle Ages.* (OM25 – IdQ 15)

> *Football and industrial history, e.g. no Wearsiders permitted to work on the Tyne (allegedly).* (MM20 – IdQ 15)

> *Traditionally competing industry (shipyards, coal miner, port activity), and much more recently, football.* (MM14 – IdQ 15)

However, what seemed to supersede these historical events in Burbano-Elizondo's attitudinal data were things like football, regional allocation of development funds and the tendency for much of the rest of Britain to consider Sunderland part of the 'Geordie' territory. For example, overwhelmingly the most frequent response placed football at the heart of the rivalry – over 93 per cent of the locals who were interviewed agreed on this.

Similar findings about the perceived dominance of Newcastle in the North-East were found among the Middlesbrough informants of Llamas's study (2001a). Comments on a perceived Newcastle bias in the regional print and broadcast media, such as, 'it should be called Tyne Tyne TV mostly cos it's very Geordie-centric', as well as comments on the economic and cultural dominance of Newcastle were frequently expressed in the attitudinal data. However, in the case of Teesside, rivalry with Newcastle/Sunderland appears to be a more recent development, coinciding with the boundary changes that 'moved' Middlesbrough out of North Yorkshire and, in terms of human geography, closer to the other conurbations in the North-East. Virtually all of the older speakers in Llamas's study expressed a dislike at being referred to as Geordie and many demonstrated a level of incomprehension at this perceived misidentification as they clearly self-identified as Yorkshire, with responses such as:

> *I'm from Yorkshire not Geordieland – they might as well call you a Frenchman instead of an Englishman.*

> *What I always say – we are the Yorkshiremen trying to keep the Geordies out of Yorkshire – cos we're on the borderlines you see.*

Although feelings towards being misidentified as Geordie were the same, such perceptions about Yorkshire were not shared by the younger informants of the study, for whom the Yorkshire label had become irrelevant to their place identity. In contrast, the majority of the middle-aged and younger speakers of the study considered themselves to be from Teesside or simply Middlesbrough. However, whether self-identifying as Yorkshire or Teesside/Middlesbrough, all informants of Llamas's study considered Middlesbrough to be part of the larger North-East region and the dominance of Newcastle in this larger region was a commonly shared perception.

In the following chapters, we will look at the similarities and differences between the varieties of English spoken in these three major urban areas of the North-East region of England with respect to pronunciation (accent), grammar and lexis.

Notes

1. Office for National Statistics website – 'Census 2001 – Sunderland'. Available at: http://www.ons.gov.uk/ons/index.html (last accessed October 2011).
2. Burbano-Elizondo (2008): Interview 2 (59:50–59:54).
3. As Burbano-Elizondo (2008) explained, for some Wearsiders, this term was created by Geordie football fans to insult their Sunderland

rivals. However, a more widely held popular story holds that the label comes from Wearside shipyards where Sunderland workers would *mak* the ships and then others would *tak 'em* away – hence 'Mackems' (Burbano-Elizondo 2008: 100).

2 Phonetics and phonology

2.1 Introduction

In the context of the vast amount of phonological variation to be found within the British Isles, the urban varieties spoken in the North-East of England are among the most easily identifiable by laypeople. Familiarity with the varieties is aided by the fact that their status and prevalence has increased considerably within the British media in recent years, and accents from the North-East are among the most frequently used localised accents on British television, particularly that broadcast at prime time. Perhaps as a consequence, these accents are generally positively evaluated and are found to be among the most socially attractive accents of British English in attitudinal surveys (see, for example, Coupland and Bishop 2007: 80).

The layperson from outside of the region may have difficulty in differentiating between varieties within the area and all accents may be perceived as 'Geordie' – the accent found in Tyneside and that associated with the major centre of gravity in the North-East, Newcastle upon Tyne. However, for inhabitants of the various urban and rural localities within and between the conurbations centred around the rivers Tyne, Wear and Tees, pronunciation differences may be perceived between localities separated by a mere few miles. In terms of vowel quality, for example, the potential confusion arising from the realisations of the NURSE[1] and NORTH vowels in Tyneside varieties is demonstrated through the well-known Geordie joke (transcribed phonetically in Viereck 1966: 95) involving a workman with an injured leg visiting a doctor to request a sick note and responding to the doctor's query of 'Can you walk?' [wɔːk] with 'Work? [wɔːk] Yer kiddin' man, I cannet even walk!' [waːk]. Such confusion, and hence the joke, would not work for speakers of Middlesbrough English, for example, where the NURSE vowel is likely to be fronted to a quality considerably closer to that of the SQUARE vowel rather than retracted to that of NORTH. Such differences are many, but yet the accents are sufficiently similar to be grouped together to constitute a dialect region labelled the 'far north' by Wells (1982), or the 'North East' by Trudgill (1990).

In this chapter we will begin by briefly describing some of the features that are used to differentiate the varieties of the north of England from both the south of England and the south of Scotland before identifying some of the phonological features that are used to differentiate the North-East from other parts of the north of England. We will then examine differences found within the North-East in both vowel quality and consonant production before briefly discussing suprasegmental features of the region and finally considering some current changes in progress for which we have evidence.

2.2 Delimiting the region

In terms of perceptual dialectology, one of the biggest divides perceived in accents of Britain concerns features which differentiate the north and the south of England. Where this division can be drawn is the subject of much debate, both academic and general. Probably the features which carry the most salience as regards indexing this division are the systemic difference of the absence of a FOOT/STRUT split and the lexical–distributional difference of the absence of BATH broadening in the north of England vs their presence in the south. In words of the FOOT class and also words of the STRUT class the /ʊ/ vowel is used in the north of England because the newer /ʌ/ phoneme, which developed from the split of the older vowel /ʊ/, is absent – so *could* and *cud*, for example, are distinguished in the south of England but not in the north of England. Older speakers may also use /uː/ in words such as *book, cook, look,* and use of /ʌ/ or a vowel which is between the two phonemes in quality such as [ə] may be found among middle-class speakers of the region, but the majority form across the north of England would be /ʊ/ in both lexical sets. In terms of BATH broadening, some would view absence of this feature as even more of a salient marker of the north of England, as Wells suggests:

> There are many educated northerners who would not be caught dead doing something so vulgar as to pronounce STRUT words with [ʊ], but who would feel it to be a denial of their identity as northerners to say BATH words with anything other than short [a]. (Wells 1982: 354)

Speakers from the north of England have retained the original short vowel /a/ which was lengthened to /ɑː/ in the south of England in most words before the voiceless fricatives /f, s, θ/, for example [gɹɑːs] *grass*, and also before certain consonant clusters containing an initial /m/ or /n/, for example [dɑːns] *dance*. In both cases speakers from the north would use the short /a/; however, there are exceptions, some of which we will discuss further in section 2.4.10. The exact geographical distribution of these two features is a matter of debate, but it need not concern us here as all varieties of our area of interest are those without the FOOT/STRUT split and without BATH broadening.

Other features can be seen as separating the far north of England from the south of Scotland. Although this linguistic separation has, at times, been seen to coincide rather unproblematically with the political border which separates the two countries, strong empirical evidence for whether this is in fact the case is only recently being examined.[2] However, as the geographical area which is the subject of this volume does not go as far north as the border we need not consider the complexity of this linguistic divide, but we can note that certain features which can be said to differentiate varieties of Scottish English from those of northern English English are unambiguously those of the latter in our area of interest, for example derhoticisation (i.e., no realisation of coda /r/ in non-prevocalic contexts), a distinction between PAM and PALM, a distinction between COT and CAUGHT, a distinction between PULL and POOL, and use of *t*-to-*r* (i.e., where *shut up* is pronounced [ʃʊɹ ʊp]).

Within the north of England, we can also attempt to delimit geographically the region of the North-East in terms of phonological features which may be present or absent and which may serve to index a general North-Eastern accent. In traditional dialectological terms, the River Tees is often seen as a boundary to the south. Harold Orton, when working on *The Linguistic Atlas of England* (Orton et al. 1978), reportedly insisted that an isogloss be drawn along the River Tees (this being the only river to have an isogloss follow it) because he knew it to be a boundary between Durham and Yorkshire (Clive Upton, personal communication). This would serve to divide the conurbation around the Tees and place Middlesbrough, which lies on its south bank, outside the North-East region. However, in modern dialect groupings, Wells (1982), Trudgill (1990) and Hughes et al. (2005) group the whole of Teesside with Tyneside in the 'north-east' or 'far north'. According to Wells, however, the accent of Tyneside differs from 'typical northern accents' considerably more than does that of Middlesbrough (typical northern accents being Greater Manchester, West Yorkshire and South Yorkshire, according to Wells (1982: 350)).

In terms of features that serve to differentiate the North-East from other northern varieties, there are more differences between the North-East of

England and varieties further south in Yorkshire than between those in the adjacent western side of the country. This is due largely to the fact of there being a lack of urban varieties directly adjacent to the North-East, and the one sizeable urban centre, Carlisle, may be said impressionistically to sound more North-Eastern than North-Western (if we take the large urban centres of the north-west of England, Manchester and Liverpool, to represent the North-West[3]). Certain features can be said to separate the North-East from other varieties of the north of England, however. The characteristic glottalisation of voiceless stops (see further section 2.5.2), the lack of definite article reduction, the use of happy tensing (i.e., the pronunciation [i] rather than [ɪ] which is found further south in Yorkshire), and use of clear final /l/s, for example, all can be said to differentiate the North-East as a region from varieties further south. A further difference can be seen in the voicing of obstruents. Yorkshire assimilation (the devoicing of syllable final voiced obstruents when they precede syllable initial voiceless obstruents either across a word boundary or within a compound word, so, for example, ['bɛttaɪm] *bed-time*), which Wells suspects is present in Cleveland[4] (1982: 367), does not appear to be so and may too be seen as a differentiator. However, in the North-East region regressive assimilation of voicing is found, so a pronunciation such as ['fʊdbɒl] *football* would be heard in the area.

These then are some of the features which can be said to characterise the North-East of England as a linguistic region as distinct from varieties to the south in Yorkshire and those to the north in southern Scotland. For our purposes we are interested primarily in the urban accents around the three industrial conurbations of Tyneside, Wearside and Teesside. Although there are considerable differences to be found between the conurbations, the similarities are such that they serve to group the varieties together as a region – at least to outsiders. Indeed, Trudgill claims:

> no one from Middlesbrough would mistake a Tynesider for someone from Middlesbrough – but the accents are sufficiently similar to be grouped together, and sufficiently *different* from those of other areas. Londoners, for instance, might mistakenly think that Middlesbrough speakers were from Newcastle, but they would be much less likely to think that they were from, say, Sheffield. (Trudgill 1990: 77)

Newcastle and Middlesbrough, then, form the geographical limits of our discussion. We have considered some ways in which these varieties are similar. We turn now to consider why it is that no one from Middlesbrough would mistake a Tynesider for someone from

Middlesbrough. In other words, we turn to an examination of the differences to be found between the urban varieties of the region.

2.3 Variation within the region

2.3.1 Perceptions of variation

The variety of the cultural and economic centre of gravity of the region, Newcastle upon Tyne, is arguably the most easily identified by outsiders. Other varieties of the North-East are customarily misperceived as Geordie by listeners from outside the region (not always to the speaker's pleasure), but varieties south of Tyneside have a number of dissimilarities from the variety of Newcastle. Middlesbrough English particularly is sufficiently different as to be also relatively commonly misperceived as Scouse – the accent associated with Liverpool. In a perceptual experiment, Kerswill and Williams (2002) found that the sample of speech from a seventeen-year-old female Middlesbrough English speaker that they presented to thirty-two adolescent judges from Hull in a dialect recognition task was much more commonly identified as Liverpool than Newcastle (eighteen of thirty-two identifications as Liverpool compared with nine identifications as Newcastle). None of the judges were able to correctly identify the accent, which demonstrates not only its unfamiliarity in general terms (unlike Geordie or Scouse) but also its hybrid nature. The history of the urban centre of Middlesbrough in terms of migration and settlement patterns may contribute to this hybridity and also to the perceived similarity of Middlesbrough and Liverpool English. In the mid-nineteenth century, the new town of Middlesbrough had a level of Irish in-migration that was second only to Liverpool at that time, with one in five adult males in the rapidly expanding steel town being Irish-born (Chase 1995). One explanation that has been proposed, then, for the perceptual similarity of these geographically separated varieties is the influence of varieties of Irish English spoken by the Irish in-migrants to these urban centres. Hickey, for example, claims:

> It is no coincidence that both Merseyside and Teesside are dialect areas of Britain which show consonant lenition and that it is these areas which had the greatest input from (southern) Irish English . . . the conclusion seems justified that the shared speech characteristics can be traced to nineteenth-century Irish migrants into these areas. (Hickey 2007: 394)

The precise similarity of the consonant lenitions mentioned by Hickey has been examined by Jones and Llamas (2003, 2008) and will be discussed further in section 2.5.2. The question of the similarity of these geographically separated varieties being the outcome of nineteenth-century dialect contact is the subject of further investigation.

Before we consider the detail of the variation to be found across the three zones of the region, we turn to a brief note on recent sources available on the accents of the North-East.

2.3.2 Sources

Compared to other regions of Britain, a wealth of relatively recent studies exists on phonological variation in the North-East. Examples of major projects which have focused on Tyneside include: the *Tyneside Linguistic Survey* (TLS), which was carried out around 1969 (Pellowe et al. 1972), *Phonological Variation and Change in Contemporary Spoken British English* (PVC), which was carried out almost thirty years later, the *Newcastle Electronic Corpus of Tyneside English* (NECTE), which combined the TLS and PVC data into a searchable database, and *Emergence of Structured Variation in the Speech of Tyneside Infants* (ESV). Data from these projects have gone on to be used in a number of publications and further studies on phonological variation, for example, from the PVC project: Docherty et al. (1997); Docherty and Foulkes (1999); Foulkes and Docherty (2000); Watt (2000, 2002); Watt and Milroy (1999); Milroy et al. (1994a, 1994b), and others; from the NECTE project: Beal (2004); Moisl et al. (2006); Moisl and Maguire (2008); Allen et al. (2006). Other studies on Tyneside English have been undertaken beyond these recent projects, for example: Beal (1985, 2000); Roach (1973); Viereck (1968) (on Gateshead English specifically); Rowe (2007), among others.

Although Newcastle English has been researched to a relatively large extent, other varieties of the North-East have not fared quite so well, though studies have been undertaken on, for example: Durham English (Kerswill 1984, 1987); Sunderland English (Burbano-Elizondo 2006, 2008); Middlesbrough English (Llamas 2001a, 2006, 2007; Jones and Llamas 2003, 2008; Watt and Llamas 2004); Darlington English (Atkinson 2011); and Newton Aycliffe English (West 2009). Additionally, Pearce (2009) has undertaken a valuable perceptual dialectological survey of the region as a whole.

A direct comparison of features is not always possible from existing literature as many different methodologies were used by these studies which had varying aims. The one large-scale survey which collected data in a systematic way from localities throughout England, the *Survey of English Dialects* (SED; Orton and Dieth 1962–71), is now over half a century old and focused primarily on rural locations, and so its utility for our purposes

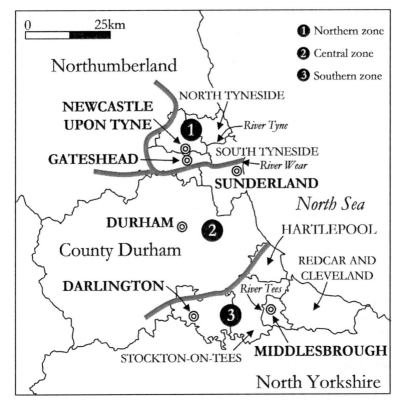

Figure 2.1 Map of perceptual areas showing three sectors (northern, central and southern, adapted from Pearce (2009))

is limited. To overcome this lack of direct comparability, a dataset which was collected specifically in order to make comparisons across some of the localities of the region is also utilised (this forms part of a larger ongoing study on variation within the North-East; see further Llamas et al. 2010). The data were collected through the use of a word list of 240 citation forms and the diagnostic reading passages the *North Wind and the Sun* and *Arthur the Rat*, and were taken from speakers from Newcastle, Gateshead, Sunderland, Durham, Darlington and Middlesbrough.

With these sources in mind, then, we turn to a consideration of some aspects of phonological variation in the region. The region will be separated into a northern zone (Newcastle, Gateshead), a central zone (Sunderland, Durham) and a southern zone (Middlesbrough, Darlington), as shown in Figure 2.1. These divisions are in line with the separations derived from around 1,600 informants' responses to the assessment of levels of 'similarity' and 'difference' between the dialects of the area in Pearce's (2009) perceptual dialectological study of the North-East.

2.4 Vowels

2.4.1 Introduction

Vowels generally carry a lot of social information and even very slight adjustments in vowel quality can cue regional as well as social differences. In terms of phonological variation, the major differences between the three zones of the North-East lie in the pronunciation of certain vowels. The vowel phonemes of the region are listed in Table 2.1.

Before taking a detailed look at the variation across the region in some of these vowels, an overall impression of the differences between Newcastle, Sunderland and Middlesbrough is given through data collected for the ongoing study mentioned above by Llamas et al. (2010). Figures 2.2–2.7 present vowel charts for six speakers (a male speaker and a female speaker from Newcastle, Sunderland and Middlesbrough) indicating the positioning of vowels after F1 and F2 measurements were taken over the mid-point of between five to ten tokens of each vowel produced in read speech. A considerable amount of variation can be seen in these data both across the localities and between the male and female speakers of the same locality (and in the case of Middlesbrough, a possible age difference).

2.4.2 FACE

The FACE vowel is one which is particularly socially sensitive and one which shows considerable variation both within communities and

Table 2.1 Vowel phonemes of the North-East region

iː	'bead'	ɑː	'bard'	aɪ	'buy'
ɪ	'bid'	ɔː	'board'	ɔɪ	'boy'
eː	'bayed'	oː	'boat'	aʊ	'cow'
ɛ	'bed'	ʊ	'bud'	iə	'pier'
ɛː	'bear'	uː	'booed'	uə	'poor'
a	'bad'	ɜː	'bird'		
ɒ	'pod'	ə	'about'		

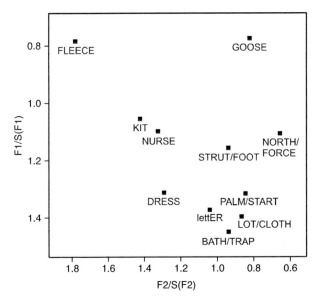

Figure 2.2 Monophthongal vowel plot for a male speaker, aged thirty-nine years, from Newcastle

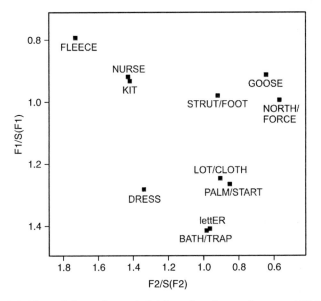

Figure 2.3 Monophthongal vowel plot for a female speaker, aged thirty-three years, from Newcastle

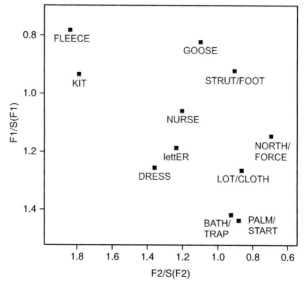

Figure 2.4 Monophthongal vowel plot for a male speaker, aged fifty-one years, from Sunderland

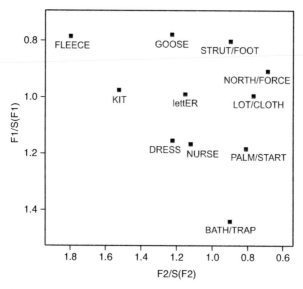

Figure 2.5 Monophthongal vowel plot for a female speaker, aged forty-two years, from Sunderland

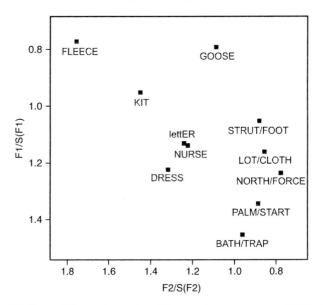

Figure 2.6 Monophthongal vowel plot for a male speaker, aged thirty-two years, from Middlesbrough

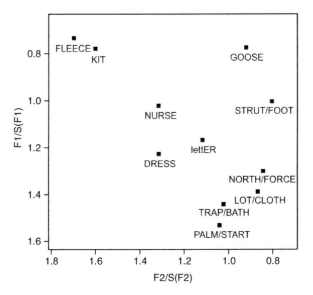

Figure 2.7 Monophthongal vowel plot for a female speaker, aged seventeen years, from Middlesbrough

Table 2.2 Variants of the FACE vowel across the three zones

Northern	eː ~ ɪə
Central	eː ~ eᵊ > ɪə
Southern	ɛ̞ː > ɪə ~ ë̞ː

across zones. A broad distribution of the variants of the FACE vowel is presented in Table 2.2.

A considerable amount of variation is in evidence in the pronunciation of this vowel. The variant which is characteristic of the region is the centring diphthong, [ɪə]. This form is to be found across the region, but is considerably less common in the southern zone than in the northern and central zones. Studies which examine variation in this vowel in socially stratified samples of speakers of Newcastle English (Watt 2000, 2002) and Middlesbrough English (Watt and Llamas 2004) have found the centring diphthong to be most associated with male speakers, and in both localities it is the preferred variant of the older working-class males specifically. The preferred form for all other age groups and for all female speakers in both of these studies is a monophthongal realisation. In the southern zone this is more open than further north, and in the data from Middlesbrough (Watt and Llamas 2004) a more centralised realisation is also to be found to a reasonably high degree in the speech of the younger females. In all localities a closing diphthongal variant – similar to [eɪ] – may be found in the speech of middle-class speakers. Such a form is to be found throughout British English.

Two exceptions are worthy of note. For the lexical items *make* and *take*, pronunciations such as [mɛk] and [tɛk] can be heard in the northern and southern zones. In the central zone, however, and specifically in Sunderland, these may be produced as [mak] and [tak]. Indeed, Beal (1993) reports that the pronunciation [mak] is believed to be the origin of the name for inhabitants of Sunderland, *Mackem*. Kerswill (1987) suggests that [mak] and [tak] are the result of lexical variation, but he reports that a style difference is in evidence in County Durham, with [a] used in informal contexts but [eː] being more frequently used in more formal situations. Another exception can be seen in the differing pronunciations of *eight, weight, straight* compared with *ate, wait, strait*. In the north and central zones, pronunciations of the former can be heard as [ɛɪ] or [æɪ] whereas the latter are produced with a variant listed in Table 2.2. In the southern zone, the same distinction applies with *eight/ ate* but the pairs *weight/wait* and *straight/strait* are homophonous.

Table 2.3 Variants of the GOAT vowel across the three zones

Northern	oː > ʊə ~ əː
Central	oː > ʊ° ~ ʊə
Southern	ɔ̞ː > ɔ̈ː ~ ɒː > ʊə

2.4.3 GOAT

The GOAT vowel is argued to vary in lockstep with the FACE vowel (see further Watt 2000), and is also important in terms of the social information it carries. Table 2.3 presents variation in the GOAT vowel across the three zones of our region.

Again, a considerable amount of variation is apparent in the realisations of this vowel both within each zone and across the region as a whole. As with the FACE vowel, the centring diphthongal variant, [ʊə], is considered a form which is localised to the North-East. It is found in all three zones of the region and, again, is associated with older working-class male speakers, but the majority form across all three zones is likely to be a monophthongal variant. As found with the FACE vowel, a difference in quality in the southern zone compared with the northern and central zones may be discerned. In varieties around the Tees conurbation, a more open quality is to be found, [ɔ̞ː]. Female speakers may produce a vowel with an even more open quality, [ɒː], as reported in Watt and Llamas (2004). A centralised form, [ɔ̈ː], is also found in Middlesbrough English. However, this form is not as fronted as the highly localised form found in varieties around the Tyne conurbation in the northern zone, [əː]. This particular form, [əː], appears to be in the process of being levelled out as discussed further in section 2.7.2. In the northern zone, as well as the localised forms (the centring diphthong and the fronted monophthong), Watt and Allen (2003: 269) report that the archaic [aː] or [aʊ] occur sporadically among older speakers in words such as [snaː] *snow* and [ˈsaʊldʒɐz] *soldiers*. Again, as with the FACE vowel, in all localities a closing diphthongal variant found throughout British English – similar to [oʊ] – may be found in the speech of middle-class speakers.

2.4.4 NURSE

The NURSE vowel also demonstrates substantial variation in the region and is also a vowel which carries considerable social information. Table 2.4 presents variation in the vowel across the three zones.

Table 2.4 Variants of the NURSE vowel across the three zones

Northern	øː ~ ɜː >ɔː
Central	ɜː > øː
Southern	ɛ̝ː > ɜː > øː

In the broadest Geordie, according to Wells (1982: 374), NURSE is merged with NORTH, so, through the influence of [ʁ] which once followed the vowel, pronunciations such as *work* [wɔːk] are heard (as noted in the introduction to this chapter). The SED records [ɔʁː] in neighbouring Northumberland. Watt and Milroy (1999) find this highly localised form to be present most commonly in the speech of older working-class males, but not as prevalent as centralised [ɜː] or the fronted [øː], the latter of which is particularly common among female speakers.

Maguire (2007), using data from traditional dialect transcriptions, the TLS and the PVC corpora, finds a merger of NURSE and NORTH to be present in the traditional dialects, though the extent of the merger both in the community and within the speech of the individuals remains unknown because of the limitations of the sampling and elicitation methods used. In the TLS corpus, which has a broader range of informants, speakers with a complete merger and those with completely distinct NURSE and NORTH lexical sets are found, though the former are the exception, which suggests a reversal of the merger (if it ever was a full merger) in Newcastle English.

In the southern zone, a fronted form is commonly found. The fronted variant, [ɛ̝ː], is particularly associated with Middlesbrough English, though it may be less common in other varieties of the southern zone. Speakers of Middlesbrough English appear very aware of this fronting and when asked whether there are features which make the accent recognisable, the fronted form of NURSE is frequently demonstrated in expressions such as *working in the works* with 'work' pronounced [wɛːk] as an example of a salient feature of the accent. This feature may be a key feature cueing the perceived similarity, noted in section 2.3.1, of Middlesbrough English with Liverpool English, which also has a characteristic NURSE/SQUARE merger at [ɛː] (Watson 2007: 358). In Middlesbrough English, the fronted form is found to be the preferred variant of the female speakers (Watt and Llamas 2004). However, contrary to what is found for the FACE and the GOAT vowel, male speakers of Middlesbrough English show a preference for the non-localisable form, [ɜː]. The young female preference for the fronted form of the NURSE vowel combined with their use of the lowered and centralised realisa-

Table 2.5 Variants of the GOOSE vowel across the three zones

Northern	uː
Central	ʉː > əu ~ ᵊu
Southern	əʉ > ʉː

tions of the FACE vowel may suggest an incipient merging of FACE and NURSE in the variety (see further section 2.7.2).

2.4.5 GOOSE

Table 2. 5 presents variants of the GOOSE vowel in the region.

In the northern zone, the GOOSE vowel is typically closer than in other parts of the region and retains a quality close to cardinal vowel 8, unlike many other accents where fronting is observed. However, in the high frequency lexical items *do* and *to* a common pronunciation of the GOOSE vowel in the north of the region can be a monophthongal realisation with the quality [i], [ɨ] or [ɪ], sometimes produced with an offglide. These forms can emerge as [ɪv] intervocalically and pronunciations such as [dɪvənt] *don't* are commonly heard, though [dɪv] without the negation clitic is rare and Rowe (2007: 361) reports it occurs only among very conservative (particularly older) speakers or among youths who self-identify as 'charvers'.[5]

In the central zone, Burbano-Elizondo (2008) reports a common perception on the part of her informants for the pronunciation of the GOOSE vowel to be a differentiator between Tyneside and Wearside English: the perceived difference being a pronunciation close to [uː] in Tyneside and one more likely to be [əu] or [ᵊu] in Sunderland. However, in her data, Burbano-Elizondo finds fronted monophthongal realisations, such as [ʉː] or [ʏː], to be more commonly used than diphthongal pronunciations. Nonetheless, the diphthongal variants are found in the recent dataset collected by Llamas et al. (2010), and a [ᵊʉ̟ː] realisation is reported for Durham vernacular by Kerswill (1987).

Varieties within the southern zone tend to have a more fronted realisation of the vowel which is commonly diphthongal. Before /l/ in words such as *school, pool, fool* etc. a triphthong, [əʉə], may be produced.

2.4.6 FLEECE

Variants of the FLEECE vowel are presented in Table 2.6.

The pronunciation of this vowel in the northern zone is commonly

Table 2.6 Variants of the FLEECE vowel across the three zones

Northern	iː ~ ei
Central	i ~ ei
Southern	ei

as a close, tense monophthong, a quality approaching cardinal vowel 1. However, in open syllables the vowel can be produced as the diphthong [ei], for example [nei] *knee*. This may also be the case before morpheme boundaries which results in distinctions such as *heed* [hiːd] and *he'd* [heid] being produced in the north of the region.

In the central zone, Burbano-Elizondo (2008: 155) reports that the FLEECE vowel is perceived by her informants as longer in Tyneside than in Sunderland and it is also perceived as having a diphthongal realisation in Sunderland as opposed to the monophthongal pronunciation which characterises the Tyneside variety for Sunderland speakers. Monophthongal variants are in evidence in the central zone, though they may be shorter in duration than those found further north. Durham English, according to Kerswill (1987: 36), lacks the distinction which depends on the presence or absence of a morpheme boundary noted above, but instead has a diphthong in all cases with the monophthongs being reserved for 'corrected' speech.

A diphthongal realisation is likely to be found most commonly in the southern zone in all contexts.

2.4.7 PRICE

Variants of the PRICE vowel are presented in Table 2.7.

Table 2.7 Variants of the PRICE vowel across the three zones

Northern	ɛi ~ ai > ei
Central	ai
Southern	ai > aːi

A regionally marked form is found in the northern zone of the region which has a high mid nucleus approximating [ei], or sometimes [ɛi], rather than the more open nucleus usually found for this vowel. This high mid nucleus is also to be found in parts of Scotland and Northern Ireland (Milroy 1995). Speakers in the northern zone may also exhibit length/quality alternations which are reminiscent of the Scottish Vowel Length Rule (see further Scobbie et al. 1999), that is, before voiced fricatives, /r/ and in final position this vowel may be longer than in other positions; so, for example, the diphthong in *knife* is shorter and has a fronter, closer onset, [neɪf], than that of *knives* [naivz] (Milroy 1995). This alternation is less likely to be found in the southern zone, however, and the realisation of the PRICE vowel is more likely to have a lower nucleus as in [ai] in all contexts.

In the northern zone, particular lexical items such as *night, right* take the FLEECE vowel, [iː], in more conservative varieties. This was found in the speech of the older male speakers by Milroy (1995) in the PVC data, but was very rare. In the southern zone, particularly before nasals, an open monophthongal vowel such as [aː] may be heard, as in, for example, the possessive pronoun *mine* [maːn].

2.4.8 MOUTH

The MOUTH vowel may be pronounced [ɛʊ] in the northern and central zones. In the south of the region the more non-localisable [aʊ] is more commonly used and the diphthong is likely to have a longer nucleus and shorter offglide than would be the case further north in the region where a shorter nucleus and longer offglide might be expected. In the northern zone a [uː] pronunciation may also be found. This is particularly common in certain lexical items which have an iconic pronunciation and act to reinforce local identity, for example [tuːn] (the pronunciation of the word *town*, but also used in the nickname of Newcastle United Football Club, *The Toon*), [bɹuːn] (the pronunciation of the word *brown*, but also the nickname of the local Newcastle Brown Ale, *Broon*).

2.4.9 THOUGHT

In THOUGHT words spelt with *a* in particular, pronunciations with [aː] may be found in the northern zone as noted in the introductory section of this chapter – so, *walk* and *talk* would be produced as [waːk] and [taːk]. This is reported as not being the case in Durham where both *walk* and *dark* would be produced with [ɑː] according to Kerswill (1987). Additionally, in the northern parts of the region, a [aʊ] pronunciation may be heard pre-<ght>, for example *daughter, thought*, and so on. Further south in the region, the more non-localisable [ɔː] would be heard.

2.4.10 *TRAP, BATH, START*

In the northern zone, a long, relatively front [aː] vowel may also be heard in words of the lexical sets TRAP and BATH, according to Wells (1982: 375), where a following voiced consonant or voiced consonant cluster are present, so *lad* would be pronounced [laːd], and *band* [baːnd], but *bath* and *rant* would take [a]. This durational difference is not found further south where [a] would be used in both cases.

As mentioned earlier, there is an absence of BATH broadening in our region, so [a] is used where lexical items in the south of England, for example, would use [ɑː] in the contexts outlined in section 2.2. An exception to this which is found throughout the North-East is in the pronunciation of *master* and *plaster* where both lexical items would be produced commonly with [ɑː]

The long back [ɑː] is also found in the northern zone in START words, such as *park* [pɑːk]. A more rounded back vowel may also be found here. In the south of the region, this is more commonly produced with a fronter vowel, such as [paːk].

2.4.11 Unstressed vowels

In the lexical sets of lettER and commA, the quality of schwa would be a fairly central [ə] in the southern zone, as found in most other parts of Britain – though a fronted variant approaching [ɛ] may also be heard reasonably commonly in the southern varieties. By contrast, in the northern zone a fairly open variant is typically used and [ɐ] is a frequent realisation of this vowel. Watt and Allen (2003: 269) also report that in Tyneside English schwa is often longer in duration than the preceding stressed syllable (even if this is a phonologically long vowel). Wells (1982: 376) notes that the quality of the lettER vowel can be very back as in [ɑ] due historically to the influence of the [ʁ] which followed it (often written as '-or' in dialect literature), though speakers may also use a front [ɛ], as heard in the southern zone, in both the lettER and commA sets in Tyneside.

In the northern and central zones, the weak vowel in *-es* and *-ed* endings, as in *horses*, *ended* and so on, are pronounced with /ə/. Further south in the region, /ɪ/ would be more common in this environment. Conversely, Wells (1982) reports that /ɪ/ would be produced in the northern zone rather than /ə/ which would appear further south in the region in words such as *seven* and *impression* [-ʃɪn].

The unstressed vowel in happY is a close [i]. The quality of the vowel may be closer to cardinal vowel 1 in the northern zone and may be longer in duration than further south in the region, but it is a tense vowel throughout the three zones.

2.5 Consonants

2.5.1 Introduction

Table 2.8 presents the consonant phonemes of the region. The consonants show much less variation across the region than the vowels of the varieties, on the whole. Nonetheless, interesting and complex differences are to be found which are discussed below.

2.5.2 /p t k/

All three of the voiceless stops can be realised as released forms, glottalled forms or glottalised forms. Glottalisation or glottal reinforcement of the voiceless stops is a salient feature of accents of the North-East. The feature is usually transcribed as a double articulation [p͡ʔ], [t͡ʔ], [k͡ʔ] or [ʔ͡p], [ʔ͡t], [ʔ͡k] and described as 'glottal masking of the oral plosive burst' (Wells 1982: 374), or 'oral closure reinforced by a glottal closure' (Gimson 1989: 159). Harris and Kaye (1990: 263) describe an intervocalic /t/ in, for example, *city*, *Peter*, as a preglottalised tap and transcribe it as [ʔɾ]. Acoustic analysis of glottalised variants of /t/, however, has led to the suggestion of [d̪] as an accurate transcription (Foulkes et al. 1999: 7; Watt and Allen 2003: 268), given the predominance of full or partial voicing and the lack of visual evidence of a glottal

Table 2.8 Consonant phonemes of the North-East region

p	'pie'	t	'tie'	k	'kite'
b	'buy'	d	'die'	g	'guy'
m	'my'	n	'nigh'	ŋ	'hang'
f	'fie'	θ	'thigh'	h	'high'
v	'vie'	ð	'thy'	tʃ	'chin'
		s	'sigh'	dʒ	'gin'
		z	'zoo'	ʃ	'shy'
w	'why'	ɹ	'rye'	ʒ	'azure'
		l	'lie'	j	'you'

stop (see further Docherty and Foulkes 1999 for detail on the acoustic features of the glottalised forms).

Though not reported in the SED, glottalisation of word-medial /p t k/ is frequently reported in the literature as a characteristic feature of Newcastle and Tyneside English (Wells 1982; Milroy et al. 1994b; Docherty et al. 1997; Watt and Milroy 1999; Watt and Allen 2003). It is also attested for Durham (Kerswill 1987), Sunderland (Burbano-Elizondo 2008) and Middlesbrough (Llamas 2007). Although glottalisation is used throughout the region, there are complex differences in the frequency of use of the glottalised forms both across the stop series and across the region.

In Newcastle and Middlesbrough, /p/ is most prone to glottalisation of the three stops. The difference between the two varieties is substantial, however, with a glottalised realisation accounting for about half of the overall sample in Middlesbrough (Llamas 2007), but around three-quarters of the overall sample in Newcastle (Docherty et al. 1997). Unlike what might be expected, Sunderland does not fall between the two according to Burbano-Elizondo's findings, where less than a quarter of the overall sample are glottalised (2008: 232). Although use of [ʔp] is more frequent in the speech of males than of females across the region, in Newcastle and Middlesbrough its use is approaching categorical for many of the male speakers whereas in Sunderland it is found to be used only 33 per cent of the time. Differences between Newcastle and Middlesbrough are much more marked in the female speech where females in Newcastle show a 58 per cent use of [ʔp] while the preferred variant of the Middlesbrough females is the released /p/, though usage of the glottalised form is increasing in the speech of the younger females (see further section 2.7.3). The female speakers of Sunderland English use a smaller amount of glottalisation than in Middlesbrough, though an increase is also noted in the speech of the younger females. Though usage is small, use of [ʔ] for /p/ is found to a greater degree in Sunderland and Middlesbrough than in Newcastle (where only a 1 per cent use for males and a 1 per cent use for females is noted). In Sunderland a 5 per cent usage is noted and in Middlesbrough a 4 per cent usage, though in Middlesbrough particularly, this usage is associated with the young female speakers (10 per cent use in young adults, 12 per cent among adolescents), which may suggest an increase in the community over time.

Of the voiceless stops, /k/ is least prone to glottalisation in Newcastle and Sunderland, but a substantial difference is observed between the two varieties in this respect. In Newcastle English, a usage of 82 per cent is recorded for male speakers and 37 per cent for females, whereas in Sunderland this is a much lower 31 per cent in male speech and 5 per cent in female speech. In Middlesbrough /k/ is more prone to glot-talisation than is /t/. As with /p/, use of the glottalised form is greater among Middlesbrough males (44 per cent) than is found in Sunderland. Use of the glottalised form among females in Middlesbrough is compa-rable to that found in Sunderland, but it is confined to the speech of the young females, which may suggest an increasing use in the community. The use of the glottal stop for /k/ is more common than the glottalised form in the female speech in both Middlesbrough and Sunderland and is found in both localities to a higher degree in the speech of the older females than the younger females, suggesting a decrease in use in the communities. [ʔ] for /k/ does not appear at all in the data from Newcastle, however. In addition to the glottalled and glottalised forms, fricated forms, that is, [x], are reasonably common in Middlesbrough English, particularly word finally. Again, this may be a feature which adds to the similarity of Middlesbrough English to Liverpool English.

As regards /t/, a considerable amount of variation is apparent which demonstrates linguistic constraints as well as geographical and social differences. Although glottal stops are virtually categorical before syl-labic L for Newcastle speakers, in word medial intervocalic position, they are less common and glottalised forms are used to a high degree in Newcastle (82 per cent male usage, 42 per cent female usage). Unlike results for /p/ and /k/, however, the overall use of the glottalised form of /t/ is higher in Sunderland English than in Middlesbrough, though use in Sunderland (38 per cent male and 10 per cent female usage) is substantially lower than that in Newcastle. The relatively low overall use of [ʔ͡t] in Middlesbrough is accounted for by the huge increase in use of [ʔ] for /t/ in the variety over apparent time (see further section 2.7.3), and among the older male speakers a 76 per cent use of [ʔ͡t] is observed, which is considerably higher than use reported for the older male speakers of the Sunderland sample (53 per cent).

In Newcastle, although glottalised forms are extremely common word internally, they are almost categorically prohibited in pre-pausal position, where released forms are preferred. Local et al. (1986: 416) argue that non-glottalised released /t/s are associated with the end of a conversational turn in Tyneside English. The phenomenon of the almost categorical realisation of /t/ as a fully released stop with no glottalisation in pre-pausal and turn-final positions has been termed the pre-pausal constraint (PPC) (L. Milroy 1997) or the final release rule (FRR) (Docherty et al. 1997). Indeed, in data from Newcastle, the FRR was found to apply 99.8 per cent of the time in word list readings and in the majority of cases in conversational data. On the rare occasion when the FRR was violated, [ʔ] appeared on tags (*isn't it?, doesn't it?, and that*) in the data. As tags are often taken to indicate the end of a turn, their turn-delimitative function is argued to be something of a Trojan horse, 'sneaking the innovatory glottal realisation into the last relevant context of the system which has hitherto resisted it' (L. Milroy 1997: 9).

In the central zone, use of released forms pre-pausally appears to be high, but whether in conversational data, the same patterns of usage as reported for Newcastle English can be found is yet to be investigated. In Middlesbrough English, the FRR is not operational and although released forms are preferred among older speakers, [ʔ] is by far the preferred form for younger males and females. /t/ > [h] may also be heard in Middlesbrough English, for example [wɒh] *what*, which, again, may give rise to a similarity between Middlesbrough English and Liverpool English. Fricated forms of /t/ are also to be found commonly word finally in Middlesbrough English and Newcastle English. Watt and Allen (2003: 268) report that the incomplete closure of [t] results in a quality similar to the Hiberno-English 'slit-t' reported by Pandeli et al. (1997). However, acoustic analysis of the fricated /t/ in Middlesbrough English and the slit-/t/ of Dublin English results in spectrally different fricatives (see further Jones and Llamas 2003, 2008).

Pre-aspiration of /t/ (and of /p/ and /k/) has been found in both Middlesbrough and Newcastle especially in the speech of young female speakers (see further section 2.7.3), and *t* > *r* is commonly found throughout the region in a restricted set of mostly monosyllabic words such as *bit, shut, put, lot*, and so on. So prevalent is it, that *t* > *r* appears in the more formal read speech in Sunderland data collected for Llamas et al. (2010).

2.5.3 /r/

The most common realisation of /r/ throughout the region is the alveolar approximant. Tapped forms of /r/ are commonly associated with the north of England, and they can still be found in the North-East, particularly in intervocalic position, though they appear to be recessive. A recent innovatory form is the labiodental approximant which is increasing in young speech both in Newcastle (Foulkes and Docherty 2000) and in Middlesbrough (Llamas 2001b) (see further section 2.7.5). The 'Northumbrian burr' [ʁ] is nowadays completely absent from urban areas and indeed very rare in rural areas, so much so that its use by speakers is said by Beal (2008: 140) to be little more than a 'party trick'. Though the uvular realisation, [ʁ], has disappeared from the urban varieties of the region, its influence can still be seen on certain vowel qualities, as noted with the NURSE and lettER vowels. Wells (1982: 374) also ascribes the [iɑ] and [uɑ]-type qualities of NEAR and CURE to its influence.

All accents of the region are non-rhotic, as noted. In linking and intrusive contexts a coda /r/ is found but, particularly in the northern zone of the region, this is produced less commonly than in other accents of England. In Newcastle English, Foulkes (1997) finds a use of linking /r/ at around 80 per cent in older middle-class speakers which drops to around 40 per cent in the speech of the young working-class cohort. Intrusive /r/ occurs around 20 per cent of the time in working-class speech, but appears to be almost completely absent in the conversational speech of the middle-class speakers. Interestingly, an increase is observed in the middle-class cohort in word list reading.

2.5.4 /h/

The northern zone of the North-East is unusual in Britain in that it is one of the few remaining urban areas where [h] is retained in words other than unstressed function words (*his, her,* etc.). Lesley Milroy reported in the late 1980s that (h) was a socially salient variable south of the River Tees but not north of it (1987: 114). However, the isogloss for this feature had, in fact, moved considerably northwards by that time. In the late 1970s and early 1980s, forensic phonetician Stanley Ellis used /h/ loss as a feature with which to identify the origins of 'Wearside Jack' – a hoax caller claiming to be 'Jack' in the case of the English serial killer, the 'Yorkshire Ripper'. Ellis reported that:

> The questioned speaker appeared to be a non-*h*-user, i.e., he dropped his initial aitches. This suggests a northern limit of the valley of the River Wear, though the actual border is not a very clear-cut one and h- might be used in some words and not in others. Certainly, if one looks as far as the river Tyne, h-sounding is the norm. (Ellis 1994: 201)

However, although Burbano-Elizondo (2008) claims that /h/-dropping is considered a shibboleth of Sunderland English of which many Tynesiders and Wearsiders are aware, her data reveal a relatively low use of /h/-dropping in her stratified sample of Sunderland English speakers (an overall rate of 11.5 per cent), with the feature being most associated with the older male speakers (a 21 per cent use recorded). Nonetheless, a distinction is maintained between Sunderland and

Newcastle English in respect of this feature as the rate of /h/-dropping is significantly higher in the former than the latter (a 4 per cent usage reported for Newcastle based on Burbano-Elizondo's analysis of six speakers from the PVC corpus).

/h/-dropping is common in the southern zone and can be seen in the pronunciation of one of the localised greetings/exclamations of the region, *howay*, which is pronounced without the initial [h] in the Tees conurbation.

2.5.5 /l/

/l/ is noticeably clear in all environments in the northern and central zones of the North-East. In the southern zone the /l/ may be less clear than further north, however. In a word like *film* where the /l/ precedes a nasal, an epenthetic vowel may be heard throughout the region, resulting in a pronunciation such as [ˈfɪləm]. This may even be produced in the more formal read speech as found in the data collected for Newcastle for Llamas et al. (2010).

2.6 Suprasegmentals

The intonation pattern of the region demonstrates less intraregional variation, and patterns are reasonably similar in the northern, central and southern zones. A characteristic feature is the use of a rise-plateau pattern found on declarative utterances (Cruttenden 1997; Watt and Allen 2003). In Tyneside English, Local (1986: 184) finds that the 'rise' is differently realised according to its placement in the tone unit and the vowel which occurs in the nuclear syllable. The rise is realised as a steady sustained rise in pitch over the syllable where the tonic syllable is final in the tone unit. However, the nuclear syllable is realised as a sustained level pitch which steps up to the next syllable which is produced with level pitch if the tonic syllable is non-final in the tone unit. In cases where there are a number of post-tonic syllables, these are produced on the same pitch level as the syllable after the tonic syllable. The rise is realised as a sustained rise in pitch over the syllable if the tonic syllable is non-final and contains a long vowel.

Newcastle English was one of a number of varieties of British English included in the Intonational Variation in English (IViE) corpus (see further Grabe et al. 2000, 2005, among others). The study recorded adolescent speakers (both males and females) from near homogeneous social groups in nine locations. Both read speech and more naturalistic speech were included in the corpus. In terms of intonation found in declarative sentences, both falls and rise plateaux patterns were found in Newcastle. The former made up the majority of the data, which were taken from a number of declarative sentences each read by six speakers. They did indicate a similarity with Belfast English, however, which showed a much higher use of the rise plateaux pattern. A wider pattern of variation was found in the production of inversion questions across dialects, with the rise plateaux pattern accounting for the majority of the utterances in Newcastle.

Truncation and compression were also investigated in four dialects from the IViE corpus: Cambridge, Leeds, Belfast and Newcastle. The stimuli consisted of the surnames *Mr Sheafer*, *Mr Sheaf* and *Mr Shift* which exhibit successively less scope for voicing. The surnames were embedded in identical carrier sentences. In producing these tokens, the speaker would either increase the rate of fundamental frequency change from the longest to the shortest word (which is compression), or complete less of the pattern (truncation). Twelve speakers from the four localities were recorded and, overall, the patterns revealed that Newcastle English, along with Cambridge English, was found to compress. The other two varieties under investigation were found to truncate (Grabe et al. 2000).

With the work from the IViE corpus and other studies mentioned above, we do have a picture of some aspects of the suprasegmental features found in Newcastle English. More work is needed to ascertain whether realisational differences such as these are found throughout the region as a whole, however, or whether significant variation exists at this level.

2.7 Current changes

2.7.1 Introduction

Recent studies which have compared the speech of the young with that of older speakers in order to infer change in progress in the community have found evidence pointing to current changes taking place in the varieties of the region. In some respects, the varieties appear to be becoming more homogeneous as highly localised forms are being used to a lesser degree in the speech of the young. In other ways, varieties can be said to be diverging or at least maintaining a level of distinctiveness as changes are adopted to differing degrees and with modifications throughout the region.

2.7.2 *FACE and* GOAT

A considerable amount of levelling appears to be taking place in the region as highly localised forms are used less commonly in communities and are to be found in the speech of the older, particularly male speakers, while pan-regional forms are used more frequently by younger speakers, particularly females. Watt (2000) has examined the levelling in lockstep of variants of FACE and GOAT in Newcastle English and found that the highly localised forms, [ɪə] for FACE and [ʊə], [ɵː] for GOAT, are used to a lesser extent among the young speakers in the PVC sample than among the older speakers, and they are associated primarily with the working-class males (see Tables 2.9 and 2.10).

This decrease in the use of centring diphthongs of both vowels ([ɪə] for FACE and [ʊə] for GOAT) among younger speakers compared

Table 2.9   Variants of FACE, all speaker groups, free conversation style (%) (Watt 2000: 78)

Group	[eː]	[ɪə]	[eɪ]	N
Older MC men	78.3	21.7	–	143
Younger MC men	73.1	14.5	12.4	145
Older MC women	90.9	2.6	6.5	153
Younger MC women	79.5	2.4	18.1	166
Older WC men	36.2	63.2	0.6	174
Younger WC men	61.5	35.9	2.6	192
Older WC women	92.6	7.4	–	121
Younger WC women	97.4	2.6	–	151

MC, middle-class; WC, working-class

Table 2.10   Variants of GOAT, all speaker groups, free conversation style (%) (Watt 2000: 78)

Group	[oː]	[ʊə]	[oʊ]	[ɵː]	N
Older MC men	72.6	12.0	–	15.4	175
Younger MC men	44.7	2.9	17.6	34.8	170
Older MC women	89.8	–	9.2	1.0	196
Younger MC women	73.7	2.9	19.9	3.5	171
Older WC men	31.6	36.2	1.7	30.5	174
Younger WC men	59.2	12.0	1.0	27.7	191
Older WC women	98.9	0.5	–	0.5	190
Younger WC women	99.5	–	–	0.5	197

MC, middle-class; WC, working-class

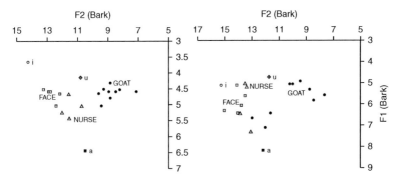

Figure 2.8 Young male speaker (left) and young female speaker (right) of Middlesbrough English (Watt and Llamas 2004)

with older speakers is found in the south of the region as well as further north (see Watt and Llamas 2004 on Middlesbrough English). In both areas an increase in use of the monophthongal forms can be observed among the working-class speakers. Despite this, differences between the north and the south of the region are not necessarily being lessened in the speech of the young, as in Middlesbrough English the quality of the monophthong for the GOAT vowel is more open and more centralised than in other varieties found further north. For the FACE vowel, the younger female speakers of Middlesbrough English particularly appear to be using an open and centralised variant which is close in quality to the pronunciation of the NURSE vowel (see Figure 2.8), which may indicate incipient merging of these vowels in the variety.

2.7.3 /p/, /t/ and /k/

As well as the levelling out of localised vowel variants, we see evidence for an increase in use of particular localised consonantal forms which results in the convergence of varieties of the southern zones with those further north. In Middlesbrough English, an increase is observed in the use of glottalised /p/ in the young speakers, particularly the young female speakers, which Llamas (2007) finds coincides with a shift in orientation in terms of local government and popular culture from south to north over the past 50 years. This movement is concomitant with a shift in speakers' sense of local identity and orientation from an alignment with Yorkshire as felt by older speakers to a more locally oriented outlook and a sense of the irrelevance of Yorkshire to place identity as felt by the younger inhabitants. Although it is suggested that this glottalisation of /p/ and /k/ may be recessive in Newcastle and is characteristic of Tyneside male speech (Docherty et al. 1997: 306), the increase in its use in the south of the region brings the urban varieties of the North-East closer in terms of overall frequency of usage and the increased use in the young female speakers of both the Middlesbrough and the Sunderland samples suggests a general convergence across the region in this feature (Middlesbrough females – 48 per cent adolescent, 12 per cent young adult, 6 per cent middle, 5 per cent older (Llamas 2007); Sunderland females – 20 per cent young, 8 per cent middle, 7 per cent older (Burbano-Elizondo 2008)).

Despite the apparent convergence in the pronunciation of /p/ across the region, the use of the glottal stop for word medial /t/, which is a much discussed spreading feature of vernacular British English, is considerably more advanced in Middlesbrough English than it is in varieties further north. This is somewhat surprising given that the form appears to be spreading from the dual epicentres of London and Glasgow/ Edinburgh (Kerswill and Williams 2000: 103) and so a higher degree of usage may be expected in Newcastle both because of its proximity to one of the epicentres and because it may be the case that the form is spreading through hierarchical diffusion, that is, spreading to larger places before smaller ones. This does not appear to be the case, however, and in the speech of the young in Middlesbrough, use of [ʔ] for word medial /t/ is approaching categorical at 89 per cent (Llamas 2007). In Newcastle English frequency of usage for this particular speaker group is considerably lower at around 11 per cent and in Sunderland it appears to be closer to Middlesbrough at 64 per cent. There is a potentially relevant time difference to be taken into account in terms of when these data were collected (Newcastle 1994–6, Middlesbrough 1998–2000, Sunderland 2003–4), but still, the differences are substantial and contribute to the maintenance of distinctiveness of varieties within the region as a whole.

In the pronunciation of word final /t/, particularly in pre-pausal position, pre-aspiration has been noted in the region. Pre-aspiration of /t/ has been observed in Newcastle English (Foulkes et al. 2005; Watt and Allen 2003) and in Middlesbrough English (Jones and Llamas 2003). It appears to be associated particularly with the speech of young females which suggests an incipient change in the region.

2.7.4 TH-fronting

Other features which are identified as current vernacular changes in British English appear to be present to a greater degree in the south of the region than further north. TH-fronting – the use of [f] and [v] for /θ/ and /ð/ respectively – is a feature which is reported to be spreading throughout the country. The association of the use of the fronted variants, [f] and [v], with child speech, combined with the fact that the use of the labiodental fricatives for the interdental fricatives involves phonemic merger, has led to the overt stigmatisation of their use. Although use of the fronted forms is reported for the north of England in the SED and earlier for Windhill in the West Riding of Yorkshire by Joseph Wright (1892), the recent rapid diffusion of the forms appears to be from the south of England northwards. In Newcastle, Watt and Milroy (1999: 30) report that the labiodental forms can be found, although they are still 'relatively scarce'. In Middlesbrough English, fronted forms of /θ/ and /ð/ are observed in the speech of young adult males (aged nineteen to twenty-two) to a high degree (over 70 per cent usage), though this is not the case for young females or adolescent males (aged sixteen to seventeen) in the sample, whose use is marginal (see further Llamas 2001b). The fronted forms are likely to be more prevalent throughout the region now, and, indeed, in data from all parts of the region analysed for forensic purposes, Peter French (personal communication) reports them to be widespread.

2.7.5 /r/

Another feature which is diffusing through British English and appears to be more common in the south of the North-East than further north is the labiodental realisation of /r/, [ʋ]. This is another feature which is associated with infantilism and it is also described as 'defective' (O'Connor 1973; Gimson 1989). Again, the variant appears to be spreading from south to north and so, perhaps as we might expect, usage in the south of the region appears to be greater than further north. In Middlesbrough English, the changes in /r/ can be seen in Figure 2.9, where we see a reduction in the use of the tapped form [ɾ] from old to young, and the appearance of the innovatory form, [ʋ], in the speech of the young adults and adolescents, with a particularly high use demonstrated by the adolescent males (39 per cent).

In their auditory analysis of labial forms of /r/ in Newcastle English, Foulkes and Docherty (2000) distinguish between a strongly articulated alveolar [ɹ], a weak alveolar [ɹ], a weak labial [ʋ] and a strongly articulated labial [ʋ]. They found that among the 334 tokens analysed, only 2 per cent of variants were classified as weak labials and 2 per cent were categorised as strongly articulated labials. The vast majority of variants produced by the sixteen young speakers in their sample were

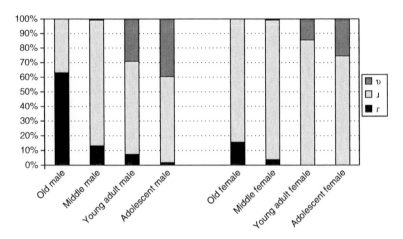

Figure 2.9 Distribution of variants of /r/ in Middlesbrough English (after Llamas 2001b)

strongly articulated [ɹ] forms (79 per cent of 334 tokens). The use of [ʋ] for /r/, then, can be regarded as an incipient sound change in the region which, though present throughout the three zones, appears to be more advanced in the southern than the central or northern zones of the region.

2.8 Conclusion

The geographical area from the north bank of the Tyne to the south bank of the Tees is regarded rather unproblematically as a dialect area, and, indeed, there is much similarity to be heard in the various accents to merit this perception. The accents of the area are distinctive and, particularly in the case of Geordie, reasonably easy for outsiders to identify. However, we have seen that a considerable amount of variation exists both within and between the accents of the urban centres of the region. The extent of homogenisation within the region is currently being assessed systematically through the ongoing study by Llamas et al. (2010), but given the strong links many of the forms may have with the distinctive identities of the region, it seems likely that, despite the similarities, some element of difference between the varieties of the North-East is likely to remain for some time to come.

Notes

1. Wells's (1982) system of referring to vowels by keywords denoting lexical sets is used throughout.

2. The ongoing project *Accent and Identity on the Scottish/English Border* (AISEB) takes four localities in the border region, two at its eastern-most point and two at the western end, and examines how variation in phonological production patterns coincides with attitudes surrounding speakers' national and regional identities and their perceptions of linguistic variation (see outputs from the AISEB project at http://www.york.ac.uk/res/aiseb/).

3. As Carlisle is one of the four localities under investigation in the AISEB project mentioned earlier, the similarities it has with varieties to the north in Scotland and to the east in the North-East of England will be assessed further and reported on in future publications.

4. Note the changing county names/boundaries in the Tees conurbation mentioned in Chapter 1.

5. A pejorative term for unruly youth.

3 Morphosyntax

3.1 Introduction

With respect to morphology and syntax, the urban varieties of English spoken in the North-East region of England share some features which are found throughout the north. The 'northern subject rule', whereby verbs take -*s* in the plural when the subject is a noun or a noun phrase, but not when it is a pronoun, is largely observed in all the varieties discussed here, as we shall see in section 3.4. Likewise, the tendency noted by Hughes and Trudgill (1979: 20) for 'auxiliary' rather than 'negative' contraction of *have, will* and *be* (e.g. *she'll not* vs *she won't*) to be more common 'the further north one goes' is to some extent borne out in the data discussed in section 3.5.3. However, the morphosyntax of North-Eastern varieties differs from that of other northern varieties in a number of respects. This is not surprising when we consider the historical factors outlined in Chapter 1. In Anglo-Saxon times, the Tees marked the boundary between the Anglian territories of Bernicia and Deira. Scandinavian settlement was denser in Deira than in Bernicia and, while, as we shall see in Chapter 4, the linguistic reflexes of this division are more evident in the area of lexis, the absence from North-Eastern varieties of what are considered characteristically 'northern' features, such as definite article reduction (Jones 2002), might have some connection with this ancient division. Since Bernicia stretched as far north as the Forth, it is not surprising that varieties spoken in the North-East of England share a number of morphosyntactic features with those of southern Scotland. As we shall see in section 3.5, this pattern is particularly striking in the area of modal and auxiliary verbs. In other respects, the three major urban varieties described in this volume differ from each other. In some cases, this is a matter of proportion, while in others, features that are found in one or two of these varieties are absent from the other(s).

In Chapter 2 we were able to exemplify the phonological features of North-Eastern varieties from a variety of spoken data sources, including conversation and read speech, The collection of data with regard to morphosyntactic features is more difficult, since, as discussed in Buchstaller and Corrigan (2011), some of these do not occur as frequently as phonological variables in interview data. In the following sections, we have therefore drawn on the results from questionnaires designed to elicit speakers' knowledge of regional morphosyntactic constructions, as well as using examples from corpora such as NECTE and reporting findings from previous investigations.

3.2 Pronouns

3.2.1 Personal pronouns

In the urban varieties of the North-East of England, personal pronouns differ from those of standard English and other regional varieties in a number of ways. These are summarised in Table 3.1, in which the pronouns which are different in the North-Eastern varieties and standard English are highlighted. As we can see, the differences are in the first and second persons, so these will be discussed in more detail. Of course, as is the case with many of the features discussed in this chapter, most speakers in the North-East of England have 'standard' as well as 'regional' forms in their repertoire and analysis of their speech reveals evidence of social, stylistic and pragmatic variation.

The first-person singular object form is often *us*, rather than *me* in North-Eastern varieties. This is used as both direct and indirect object, as in the following examples (in all cases, it is clear from the context that the speaker is referring to him- or herself alone).

Oh, thanks pal. Thanks, you're the first person that's give us a tip. (NECTE)

Our Mark calls us gramma. (Sunderland interviews – Burbano-Elizondo 2008)

Lend us your catalogue – I want to have a flick through it. (Language questionnaire, Llamas 1999)

Give us me shoe back. (Snell 2007: 55)

Snell found in her study of children's usage on Teesside that first-person singular *us* was used exclusively in imperatives, as in the example above, and that this feature had the pragmatic function of mitigating the face-threatening nature of the imperative. The examples from Tyneside and Sunderland above demonstrate that, in these dialects, singular *us* is not restricted to imperatives. When the pronoun is conjoined with a noun, *me* rather than *us* is used, as in the following:

They used to lock me and my mum in the top bedrooms. (NECTE)

Table 3.1 Personal pronouns in Tyneside, Wearside, Teesside and standard
English

Person/ number/ case	Tyneside	Wearside	Teesside	Standard English
1st singular subject	I	I	I	I
1st singular object	us	us	us	me
1st singular possessive	me (/mi/)	me (/mi/)	me (/mi/)	my
2nd singular subject	ye	ye	ye	you
2nd singular object	you	you	you	you
2nd singular possessive	your	your	your	your
3rd singular subject	he/ she/it	he/ she/it	he/ she/it	he/ she/it
3rd singular object	him/her/ it	him/her/ it	him/her/ it	him/her/ it
3rd singular possessive	her/his/ its	her/his/ its	her/his/ its	her/his/ its
1st plural subject	we	we	we	we
1st plural object	we (/wə/)	us	us	us
1st plural possessive	wor	our	our	our
2nd plural subject	yees/ yous/you	Yous/you	Yous/you	you
2nd plural object	yous/you	You	Yous/you	you
2nd plural possessive	your	your	your	your
3rd plural subject	they	they	they	they
3rd plural object	them	them	them	them
3rd plural possessive	their	their	their	their

Table 3.1 shows the form *me* for first-person singular possessive in all three North-Eastern varieties. Use of this variant is by no means confined to the North-East: Kortmann and Szmrecsanyi (2004: 1153) show that it is widespread within and beyond the British Isles. Nevertheless, Snell (2010) argues that it is locally salient in the North-East and demonstrates how children in Teesside exploit variation between standard

my and regional *mi* forms of the first-person singular possessive in their everyday interaction.

In the first-person plural, some North-Eastern varieties have a limited form of 'pronoun-exchange', with *we* (/wə/) used for the object form. This contradicts the view stated in Ihalainen (1994: 231) that pronoun-exchange is confined to western dialects of English. This form has been found in data from Newcastle and Sunderland, but not from Middlesbrough. An example is:

You can come with we to that as well. (NECTE)

In Tyneside English, the first-person plural possessive pronoun may be realised as *wor*, as in the following example:

Wor Thomas'll be fourteen on Christmas Day, and wor little Steven, that's the seventh; he'll be ten. (NECTE)

Burbano-Elizondo's Sunderland informants identified this as a 'Geordie' feature, and it has not been found in data from Middlesbrough. In Wearside and Teeside, the form is more likely to be *our*, but all three North-Eastern varieties share a tendency for the first-person plural form to be used with reference to family members and sexual partners. Examples of this are:

Our lad was asking after you. (Sunderland – referring to the speaker's brother) (Burbano-Elizondo, unpublished data)

Our mam. (Middlesbrough – where the speaker is an only child) (Llamas, unpublished data)

Wor lass was drinking purple passions all night. (NECTE – referring to the speaker's girlfriend)

In standard English, the paradigm of second-person pronouns is reduced to just two forms: *you* and *your.* While earlier English and other European languages mark these pronouns for both case and number, these distinctions had disappeared from standard English by about 1700. Most regional varieties in the north of England either retain the earlier second-person singular forms *thee/ thou/ thy* or use the innovatory plural form *yous.* The former is more common in the north-west and south of the Tees, though the SED shows it being used in County Durham. Speakers of the urban varieties described in this volume are more likely to use either the standard English forms, or analogically created plural forms such as *yous.* The ultimate origin of forms like *yous* is probably Irish English, since Wright (1896–1905) includes examples from Ireland, but none from England, Scotland or Wales. As we have seen in Chapter 1, all three conurbations had a considerable influx of Irish immigrants in the nineteenth century, which might support the idea of an Irish English origin for *yous* in the North-East, but Cheshire et al. (1993) argue that this form is spreading throughout urban areas of Britain. Thus, it is found in Edinburgh as well as Glasgow even though it is the latter city that experienced high levels of Irish immigration. For the second-person singular subject form, Tyneside and Sunderland retain the *ye* form found in Northumberland by the SED fieldworkers. Examples of these second-person forms are:

Well ye haven't got any. (NECTE)

Yous'll have Thomas next year. (NECTE – referring to the whole class)

There's a job going at our place if youse two want to go for it. (Llamas 1999)

He says 'ye're left-handed', you know. (Sunderland interviews – Burbano-Elizondo 2008)

Some of Burbano-Elizondo's informants argued that *thou* could be heard in Sunderland but none of them actually used it in the interviews. Some identified it more with Durham, 'pitmatic' (in this case referring to the dialect of the Durham coalfield) and the usage of older speakers in Sunderland.

Table 3.1 shows no difference between standard English and North-Eastern varieties in the forms of third-person pronouns. However, the object form is used in subject position when this is either conjoined or when it is separated from the verb or is emphatic, as in the following examples:

Me and my mam and dad are going out for a meal. (NECTE)

I think she likes getting bathed her. (NECTE)

Her and her son are still living there. (NECTE)

You know, her that's always late. (NECTE)

3.2.2 Relative pronouns

In standard English, relative clauses can be introduced by the '*wh*-relatives' (*who, whom, whose,* or *which* according to case and animacy), by *that*, or they can simply follow the antecedent clause without any overt marking (zero). The last option tends not to be used when the antecedent is the subject, and *that* is less common when the antecedent is animate. *That* is not used when the relative clause is unrestricted or parenthetical. In her sociohistorical study of relative clauses, Romaine demonstrates that the '*wh*-relatives' entered the written language 'from above' and suggests that 'infiltration of WH into the relative system . . . has not really affected the spoken language' (1982: 212).

In the traditional dialects of the north of England, as exemplified in the *Survey of English Dialects* (SED; Orton and Dieth 1962–71), the '*wh*-relatives' (*who, which*) are not used at all where the antecedent is subject. The question designed to elicit subject relative constructions was:

> *The woman next door says: The work in this garden is getting me down. You say: Well, get some help in. I know a man . . . will do it for you.*

In Northumberland, in five locations, the zero (Ø) strategy was used, that is, 'a chap would do it'; in three *at* was used; and in one location *that* was used. On the other hand, the SED responses to the question eliciting the genitive relative reveal some use of *whose*, especially in Northumberland and Durham. In response to the question *That man's uncle was drowned last week. In other words, you might say, that's the chap . . .*, *wh*- in the form of /hwe:z/ or /wi:z/ was given in seven locations in Northumberland, 'at his uncle was . . .' in one location and 'as his uncle was . . .' in the remaining one location. The use of *what* as a relative marker was not attested in Northumberland or County Durham in the SED materials, and Kortmann (2008: 491) includes this in a list of definitively southern English features. He does, however, note that relative *what* is now used in the north of England, which corroborates Cheshire et al.'s statement that 'relative *what* was reported just as frequently in . . . the North of England as in the South . . . *What*, then, appears to be the preferred relative pronoun in the urban centres of Britain today' (1993: 68). Although relative *what* is attested in North-Eastern varieties, it is still not used as frequently here as further south. Beal and Corrigan (2005a), comparing results from NECTE and a corpus of Sheffield English also collected in the second half of the twentieth century, found *what* to be much rarer in the former than in the latter. However, as the following examples demonstrate, *what* is used in all three urban dialects of the North-East:

> *Bairns don't play the games what we did.* (NECTE)

> *That's the best one what she's got on.* (Llamas 1999)

> *That's all what I've put, 'bright'.* (Sunderland interviews – Burbano-Elizondo 2008)

In an earlier study (2002), Beal and Corrigan found that, while the oldest speakers in the NECTE corpus (born in the late nineteenth century) showed patterns similar to those of SED informants from Northumberland, there was a sharp increase in the use of *wh*-relatives by NECTE speakers born in the 1920s and 1930s, and that the youngest speakers (born in the 1970s) tended to use *wh*-, *that* and *zero* forms in more or less equal proportions. This would suggest that Romaine's statement cited above is no longer valid, since *wh*-relatives have now 'infiltrated the spoken language' in the North-East of England. Nevertheless, it is still the case that constructions are attested from this area which would not be found, or at least not found as frequently, in standard English. The zero relative construction is still used where the antecedent is in subject position, as the following examples illustrate:

> *I've a sister 's over there, she loves stotties.* (NECTE)
>
> *There's about twenty of them are walking along.* (NECTE)
>
> *Then there's the shipyards was going strong then as well.* (Sunderland interviews – Burbano-Elizondo 2008)

There are also examples of *that* being used when the relative clause is unrestricted or parenthetical, as in the following:

> *The old grammar school on Durham Road, that was a co-educational school.* (NECTE)
>
> *This is Louise, that was meant to come.* (NECTE)
>
> *Most of them took a redundancy, that was fifty and over.* (Sunderland interviews – Burbano-Elizondo 2008)

In the first of these examples, *that* is unstressed and so cannot be a demonstrative, while in the second and third it is clear that a specific person or persons is/are being referred to. In all cases, *wh*- forms would be required in standard English.

3.3 Definite and indefinite articles

3.3.1 The definite article

As we saw in section 3.1, although definite article reduction, whereby *the* is reduced to /t/ or a glottal stop, is considered to be 'perhaps the most stereotypical feature of northern British English dialects' (Jones 2002: 325), these reduced forms are not found north of the Teesside conurbation. Here, the full form of the definite article is the norm. What marks

North-Eastern varieties out as distinct from standard English and many other English (but not Scottish) dialects is the range of contexts in which the definite article is used. These contexts include kinship terms (a wider range than the ubiquitous *the wife*), names of institutions, seasons, illnesses and even numbers. Examples are:

Going over to the girlfriend's concert first though. (NECTE)

I think Karen and Kell are going down there the night. (NECTE)

So I never really started work 'til I was about the fifteen. (NECTE)

Well, I've got a little laddie that gans to the Beacon Lough. (NECTE – 'Beacon Lough' here refers to a school)

Because he'll not sleep the night. (Sunderland interviews – Burbano-Elizondo 2008)

3.3.2 The indefinite article

In Tyneside and Wearside, the indefinite article is used with *one*, as in the following examples:

It was a one that was a good stinger to get them out of the way. (NECTE)

That's right yes, there's a one coming. (NECTE)

'Heed' is a one for Sunderland. I don't use it. (Sunderland interviews – Burbano-Elizondo 2008)

A one German was telling us . . . (Sunderland interviews – Burbano-Elizondo 2008)

In standard English and most other dialects, the first of these sentences would be ungrammatical and an adjective would need to be placed between *a* and *one* to make the second grammatical, e.g. *there's a new one coming.*

3.4 The northern subject rule

Traditionally, all northern English dialects observe the 'northern subject rule', for which Kortmann provides the following formulation: 'every verb in the present tense can take an *s*-ending . . . unless its subject is an immediately adjacent simple pronoun' (2008: 482). Beal and Corrigan (2000) found that this rule still operates in Tyneside English. Examples of the -*s* form with plural nouns are:

Our young one's mates talks something like you. (NECTE)

Examples of verbs without -*s* after simple pronouns include:

We visit her mam. (NECTE)

Beal and Corrigan (2000) found that the constraint against using the -*s* form after simple pronouns was particularly strong, but the use of -*s* after plural noun subjects was found to be more common after conjoined nouns, as in:

Aye, and your sister and your mam comes out. (NECTE)

3.5 Negation

In her account of Tyneside and Northumbrian English, Beal (1993) notes the following ways in which patterns of negation in these North-Eastern varieties of English differ from those in standard English:

1. *Never* is used as a punctual negator with verbs in the past tense, used for emphasis rather than with the meaning 'not ever'.
2. Negative concord (the 'double negative' is used).
3. Auxiliary contraction (e.g. *he'll not, she's not, they're not*) is more common than in standard English.
4. The modals *can* and, more rarely, *will* have uncontracted negative forms *cannot, winnet*.
5. There is a complex system of interrogative tags, in which, for example, *can't she not?* seeks confirmation of a negative; *can't she?* seeks confirmation of a positive and *can she not?* simply seeks information.
6. The negative of auxiliary *do* has local forms such as *divvent*.

Some of these patterns can be found in other northern dialects, or even in non-standard English more generally, while others are more restricted to the North-East within England, though they are also found in Scotland.

3.5.1 Punctual never

This feature is by no means restricted to North-Eastern varieties of English. Cheshire et al. note that '*never* as a past tense negator was among the most widely reported features' in the results of their nation-wide survey of non-standard grammar (1993: 67). *Never*, when heading a verb in the past tense as in *I waited all night but you **never** came* is perfectly acceptable standard English usage: the non-standard use of *never* as a negator is restricted to phrases containing a verb referring to a single action or a delimited span of time. Thus the following examples would be deemed non-standard:

Now this house here has never been done since we come in. (NECTE)

He never dropped like a set . . . against anybody. (NECTE – referring to a specific tennis match)

They said they were coming back on Monday and they never. (Llamas 1999)

I never wrote that down. (Sunderland interviews – Burbano-Elizondo 2008 – referring to a single occasion)

3.5.2 Negative concord

According to Hughes et al., negative concord, or 'multiple negation' is one of the 'grammatical forms which differ from those in Standard English and which can be found in most parts of the British Isles . . . because . . . it is, in fact, the standard dialect which has diverged from the other varieties' (2005: 22). However, there are studies which indicate that negative concord may, in fact, have a regional distribution within Britain. Kortmann states that 'multiple negation is far more frequently used in the South than in the North of England' (2008: 483); Cheshire et al. note that 'multiple negation was reported less frequently in the North of Britain than in the Midlands, and most frequently in the South' (1993: 76); and Anderwald (2002) broadly confirms this regional distribution. In Anderwald's study, which is based on the *British National Corpus* (BNC) and therefore only includes data from highly educated speakers, the North-East is the exception to this rule, having 20.5 per cent of tokens with negative concord compared to 9.7 per cent for the north as a whole. In a study based on a sample of the NECTE corpus, Beal and Corrigan (2005b) contradict Anderwald's findings. They found negative concord to be much rarer in NECTE than in the BNC subcorpus, occurring in only 6 per cent of possible cases (5/82 tokens). When they examined the distribution of these five tokens of negative concord, it became clear that the use of this feature is socially rather than regionally distributed: the speakers who use negative concord are all male and working class, having left school at the legal minimum age of fifteen. All three speakers use negative concord while explicitly stating that the education system failed them:

They never learned you nowt you were wasting your time.

Education as far as jobs gan just now, doesn't count for nowt. Wey it counts for a very little like.

They said I was too clever, they went and jumped us two classes, and I was never no good after that.

Although no quantitative studies of negative concord in Wearside and Teesside have yet been carried out, positive responses to the following item in Llamas's (1999) grammar questionnaire study indicate that it is common in Teesside:

They can't do nothing without you saying. (Llamas 1999)

3.5.3   Auxiliary contraction

Unlike negative concord, which is highly stigmatised and, at least in the NECTE corpus, largely confined to less educated working-class male speakers, auxiliary contraction is regionally rather than socially distributed. Hughes and Trudgill suggest that, within Britain, the tendency to use auxiliary contraction increases 'the further north one goes' (1979: 20). Although Tagliamonte and Smith's (2002) comparison of data from a range of British dialects broadly contradicts this finding, their corpus from Wheatley Hill, County Durham, displayed one of the highest percentages of auxiliary contraction (45 per cent). This was close to the figures from their Scottish corpora from Cumnock (51 per cent) and Buckie (38 per cent) and from their Northern Irish data from Cullybackey (42 per cent). So, while Tagliamonte and Smith's findings do not support Trudgill's suggestion of a north–south cline, they do demonstrate that auxiliary contraction is common in the North-East of England, and that, in this respect, dialects from this part of England are more like those in Scotland and Northern Ireland than their English neighbours to the south. Anderwald, like Tagliamonte and Smith, finds no clear north–south pattern in the distribution of auxiliary contraction, noting that 'Scotland does indeed behave significantly differently from the rest of Britain' but otherwise 'in the north-south direction there are no other cross-cutting significance boundaries' (2002: 76). However, again like Tagliamonte and Smith, Anderwald provides figures for the North-East of England that are very similar to those from Scotland. Both Tagliamonte and Smith and Anderwald note that with the verb *be* auxiliary contraction is more common than negative contraction in all dialects. Tagliamonte and Smith also point out that they found only negative contraction in tag questions, and that negative contraction was much more common with *have* (2002: 264, 268).

In their small-scale study of data from the NECTE corpus, Beal and Corrigan (2005b) found patterns of auxiliary contraction similar to those from Tagliamonte and Smith's Wheatley Hill data. Negative contraction was more common with *have*; auxiliary contraction was much more common with *be* (86.74 per cent auxiliary contraction vs 13.25 per cent negative contraction); only negative contraction was used in tags; and, with regard to negated *will*, 71.4 per cent of tokens in Beal and Corrigan's study had auxiliary contraction, compared to 70 per cent in Tagliamonte and Smith's Wheatley Hill data. This suggests that, although Trudgill's statement that auxiliary contraction is more common 'the further north one goes' needs to be qualified, it is certainly characteristic of dialects in the North-East of England. Examples of auxiliary contraction are:

Oh no we have no attachments, but it's not a case of leaving it. (NECTE)

They're not worth voting for. (NECTE)

My mother and father were born in Gateshead, but er I'll not gan into that like. (NECTE)

The teacher'll not tell them. (NECTE)

Because he'll not sleep the night. (Sunderland interviews – Burbano-Elizondo 2008)

Although this feature was not included in Llamas's (1999) question-naire, it is also found in Teesside.

3.5.4 Uncontracted negatives

In standard English, uncontracted forms of the negative are used for emphasis and, in such cases, the word *not* is stressed. Examples of this would be:

*You can **not** be serious!*

*I will **not** do that!*

In North-Eastern varieties, uncontracted forms of *can* and, more rarely, *will* occur with no stress on *not* and with the vowel in the final syllable pronounced as /ə/ or /ɪ/. Although Beal and Corrigan (2005b) found no examples of this, McDonald (1981: 126) had one example of *winnet* in her corpus of Tyneside/Northumbrian English:

> *I winnet empty the pedal bin.*

Beal and Corrigan found uncontracted *cannot* in their data, albeit not in a majority of cases: 79.74 per cent of tokens of negated *can* had *can't* as opposed to 20.25 per cent with *cannot*. For some speakers at least, the two forms are interchangeable, even occurring within the same utterance:

> *You can't change that. Cannot do anything about it.*

Other examples of *cannot* from Tyneside and Sunderland include:

> *And now old people cannot get a job.*
>
> *If you speak Tyneside, they'll not answer you back for the simple reason they cannot understand you.*
>
> *I cannot remember him ever hitting me.*
>
> *[In] Durham, you cannot predict whether someone is gonna be a Geordie or a Mackem.* (Sunderland interviews – Burbano-Elizondo 2008)
>
> *Have a look! It seems that you cannot find anything.* (Sunderland interviews – Burbano-Elizondo 2008)
>
> *I cannot really write it.* (Sunderland interviews – Burbano-Elizondo 2008)

Llamas has no evidence of uncontracted *cannot* in her Teesside data, so this may be a feature that differentiates this variety from the other urban dialects of the North-East.

3.5.5 *Interrogative tags*

McDonald (1981) describes a complex system of negative interrogative tags operating in the grammar of Tyneside/ Northumbrian English. According to McDonald, a negative clause followed by auxiliary + subject + not is used when information is sought, as in:

> *She can't come, can she not?*

When confirmation of the negative is sought, a negative clause followed by auxiliary + n't + subject + not is used, as in

> *She can't come, can't she not?*

This pattern is also used in negative questions, where the speaker knows very well that the answer is *no*, but requires confirmation, possibly to settle a dispute with a third party. It is often used by children appealing to adult arbitration. An example would be:

Can't Jack not swim?

Here, what is implied is that everybody knows that Jack cannot swim, but Jack is denying this. A similar contrast occurs between two patterns for negative tags following positive clauses, with auxiliary + subject + not used when asking for information, and auxiliary + n't + subject, when confirmation is sought instead. Examples of these would be:

She can come, can she not?

She can come, can't she?

The examples above are all taken from McDonald and Beal (1987), which provides a summary of McDonald's (1981) thesis. The schema outlined here was devised on the basis of elicitation experiments rather than derived from corpus data alone. Indeed, given the very specific pragmatic contexts required for each of these options, it would be very difficult to find sufficient tokens in a corpus. Beal and Corrigan (2005b) found this to be the case when they searched in vain for tokens in NECTE. They did, however, find some tokens of interrogatives with uncontracted negatives:

Yes, well do you not think it's come more popular since these er Mike Neville and George House on the telly?

Do you know where that case of Brown-Ale is? Do you not?

Have you not kept that, have you not kept that?

In all of these, there is an element of surprise or exasperation, suggesting that the uncontracted negative in an interrogative or tag has some kind of emphatic force.

3.5.6 Local forms of negated do

In the North-East of England, there are negative forms of *do* which are not found in other parts of England (though they are found in Scotland). In Tyneside, the local form is *divvent/ divn't*, while in Sunderland *dinnet* is also found. The latter could be considered an uncontracted negative like those discussed in section 3.5.5, but attitudinal evidence suggests that forms of *do* are more locally salient. A search of the NECTE corpus revealed that, if we count all tokens of *divven't, doesn't* and *don't* (*didn't* can be excluded as *divvent* is less likely to be used in past tense contexts), *divvent* accounts for 6.82 per cent of all tokens of non-past tense negated *do* (170 tokens of *divvent* against 2,066 of *don't* and 256 of *doesn't*). However, just over half the speakers in the NECTE corpus have no tokens of *divvent*, while others use it frequently. TLSG37 has twenty-one tokens of *divvent* against six of *don't* and no tokens of *doesn't* (77.77 per cent). This is the most extreme example, but others show relatively high use of *divvent*. TLSG27 has 36.36 per cent *divvent* and TLSG30 has 30.76 per cent. These speakers were all recorded in 1969 for the *Tyneside Linguistic Survey*, but the overall rate of use of *divvent* is not much lower in the PVC subsection of NECTE (recorded in 1994): overall PVC speakers have 6.17 per cent tokens of *divvent* against 7.27 per cent for TLS, so we cannot infer that *divvent* is becoming less frequent. Indeed, some of the most frequent users of *divvent* in the PVC subcorpus are young male speakers. Many, though by no means all of the tokens of *divvent* occur in the phrase *I divvent know* (where *know* is often pronounced /na:/), so it could be the case that a very localised form is being preserved because of its occurrence in a frequently used phrase. Frequent users of *divvent* also tend to be male and/or working class, so, like multiple negation, this feature appears to be socially stratified. Examples of *divvent* from the NECTE corpus include:

I divn't suppose he ever come back.

Well, divn't ask me for any.

I divn't gan for holidays man.

I divn't know nothing about that.

No examples of *divvent* or *dinnet* have been found in data from Teesside. Evidence of a dialect difference between Tyneside and Wearside was recorded by Burbano-Elizondo (2001: 119) in her study of lexical variation in two groups of secondary-school students. In this study, whereas the Tyneside group identified *divvent* as a local feature, *dinnet* was only elicited as a local feature among the Sunderland student group. The saliency of this difference became clear in the responses that Sunderland speakers from all age groups provided to the language questionnaire administered by Burbano-Elizondo (2008) for her study of language variation and identity in Sunderland. To date, however, no systematic analysis of *dinnet* has been conducted in the conversational Sunderland data available. It is a feature that is indeed present in Burbano-Elizondo's (2008) conversational data; however, based on initial reaction to such data, we can tentatively argue that usage of this local verb form does not appear to be much more frequent than the rates reported for *divvent* in the TLS and PVC corpora (see above). Examples of *dinnet* from Burbano-Elizondo's corpus are the following:

> *You know where 'brass' comes from dinnet ya?* (Sunderland interviews – Burbano-Elizondo 2008)

> *I'm a Wearsider but I dinnet mind being call 'Mackem' [. . .] but I'm definitely not a Geordie.* (Sunderland interviews – Burbano-Elizondo 2008)

Given that, for Burbano's Sunderland participants at least, *divvent* is indexed as 'Geordie' and *dinnet* as 'Mackem', this could be a feature that, perceptually at least, differentiates the three major urban varieties in the North-East from each other.

3.6 Modal verbs

Beal (2008: 386) suggests that 'the system of modal verbs in the North-east, especially Tyneside and Northumberland, is more like that of Scots than that of Standard English and English dialects in the South and Midlands'. Some of these distinctive modal constructions, notably the 'double modal' (section 3.6.3) are recessive and increasingly less likely to be heard or recognised even on Tyneside, let alone Sunderland and Middlesbrough. Others, such as epistemic *must*, discussed in section 3.6.2, are more robust throughout the North-East, but can also be found elsewhere in the north of England. Since the pragmatic conditions needed for modal constructions may not arise in interviews or recorded conversations, much of the information in this section has been taken from the results of questionnaires designed to elicit recognition and acceptability of constructions.

3.6.1 Range of modal verbs

The core modal verbs in standard English are *can, could, may, might, must, shall, should, will* and *would*. Even in standard English, there have been changes in the use and distribution of these forms: *will* or the reduced form *'ll* is increasingly used instead of *shall* and *can* is taking over the 'permission' sense of *may* (see Mair 2006: 100–3 and Denison 1998: 165 ff. for further discussion of recent changes in standard English). In the North-East of England, these trends are more advanced. The NECTE corpus has only five instances of *shall*, all of which occur in first-person questions:

> *Shall I rattle on while you're doing it?*
>
> *Shall we go down to the woods today?*
>
> *Shall I see if I can sort something out tonight for you?*
>
> *Shall I say the one nearest or go on to eh the last one?*
>
> *Shall we say we talk King's English with a slight accent?*

This is the only context in which *will* is not found in standard English, but in Tyneside English, although, as the examples above demonstrate, *shall* is used in first-person questions, *will* is also acceptable (McDonald 1981).

May is likewise rare in the NECTE corpus, though, with seventeen tokens, it is more frequent than *shall*. Six of these instances have either *well* or *as well* in close proximity to *may*, as in the examples below:

> *The general feeling is what they're doing may well be based on some realistic fact.*
>
> *I decided to do English because I thought I may as well do what I like best.*
>
> *I thought well I may as well do my training if I can.*

There are no instances of permissive *may* in NECTE: all seventeen tokens involve possibility. Even in this sense, the speakers in NECTE are much more likely to express possibility with *maybe* or *maybes* than with a modal verb, as in the following examples:

> *I lived in there for about eighteen or nineteen year maybe a little bit longer.*
>
> *Different nights I maybe stop in as I say watch the telly different nights maybe go to the club one night you know but eh the only thing I would change is eh sports wise you know maybe learn golf or learn another sport you know.*

The marginal modal *ought (to)* is even rarer than *shall* in the NECTE corpus. Only one token occurs in the speech of participants:

> *I think I ought to make a speech.*

In the TLS part of the NECTE corpus, the interviewer sometimes uses *ought* in questions to the participants, but they never use it in their responses, as the following exchange shows:

> <How do you feel about equal pay for women do you think women ought to get equal pay for equal work?>
>
> *I think some sometimes they should.*

This suggests that, even in the pragmatic contexts in which *ought* is used in standard English, this verb is avoided in Tyneside English and *should* carries the meaning of obligation instead.

3.6.2 Epistemic must

In standard English, positive *must* can either be used epistemically, to express a conclusion, or with the meaning of obligation, but negative *mustn't* is only used in the latter sense. In North-Eastern dialects of English, *must* is used to express conclusions rather than obligation in both positive and negative clauses. Examples are:

> *She was, she . . . must have been drunk.* (NECTE)
>
> *The lift mustn't be working.* (McDonald and Beal 1987)

In North-Eastern dialects, obligation is expressed by *have to* or *(have) got to*, as in the following examples from NECTE.

> *They have to keep . . . extending and that.*
>
> *We've got to stay awake.*
>
> *Well you played the game, you got to pay the consequences.*

One consequence of this preference for *(have) got to* in the sense of obligation, is that the negative *haven't got to* means 'obliged not to' rather than 'not obliged to' in the North-East. Thus *You haven't got to open the door* is the equivalent of standard English *You mustn't open the door* rather than *You are not obliged to open the door.*

3.6.3 Double modals

In standard English and most other dialects in England, only one modal verb can appear in a single verb phrase. Thus, *He must be able to do it* is 'grammatical' while *He must can do it* is not. In some North-Eastern dialects of English, this rule does not apply so long as the second modal is *can* or *could*, so the asterisked sentence would be grammatical in these dialects. More combinations of modals are allowed in Scots than in North-Eastern English dialects, and more are allowed in the dialect of rural Northumberland than in that of urban Tyneside. Examples from McDonald (1981: 186–7) are:

> *I can't play on a Friday. I work late. I might could get it changed, though.*

> *The girls usually make me some (toasted sandwiches) but they mustn't could have made any today.*

> *He wouldn't could've worked, even if you had asked him.*

While these double modal constructions are found in Scots and in some dialects of the southern USA, the only area of England in which they occur is the North-East. Even here, they are rare and probably recessive: the only example found in the NECTE corpus is:

> *You'll probably not can remember, but during the war there wasn't wool.*

Of course, the pragmatic contexts in which double modals can occur are rare, and unlikely to arise in interviews. However, elicitation tests do seem to confirm that double modals are recessive in the North-East of England. McDonald (1981) found that 15.42 per cent of respondents from north of Durham found sentences with double modals wholly acceptable and normal or somewhere between this and unacceptable. In a later survey, Beal and Corrigan (2000) found that only 9.37 per cent of a sample of sixteen- to seventeen-year-olds from Bedlington, Northumberland, found the same sentences either 'natural' or 'familiar', while 90.63 per cent found them 'alien'. The acceptability of the constructions was higher among working-class children, who may well still hear them used by their grandparents.

Both Burbano-Elizondo (2008) and Llamas (1999) included an example of a double modal construction in their questionnaires. In both cases, no informant ticked the box to indicate that they were familiar with or would use the construction, and the Sunderland participants stated that the examples did not make sense. This confirms the findings of McDonald (1981) and Beal and Corrigan (2000) that the double modal construction is receding northwards. It is now very rare in Tyneside and apparently unknown in Sunderland or Middlesbrough.

3.7 Conclusion

It is clear from the discussion above that there is a great deal of research still to be undertaken on the morphology and syntax of varieties of English in the North-East of England. More examples have been provided from Tyneside than from Wearside or Teesside because there is no searchable database of the latter two varieties comparable to the NECTE corpus. Where no example of a construction from Sunderland or Teesside is given, this does not necessarily mean that the construction would not be found in these dialects. Nevertheless, the elicitation data obtained by Burbano-Elizondo and Llamas does provide some pointers to similarities and differences in the morphosyntax of these three varieties. All three have features found elsewhere in the north of England, such as the 'northern subject rule', but on the other hand all three are distinct from other 'northern' varieties of English in having no definite article reduction. Although the traditional dialects of County Durham retained the second-person singular pronoun *thou*, all three urban varieties in the North-East have abandoned this, and instead have the option of using more innovative second-person plural forms such as *yous*.

In some respects, there seems to be a cline of 'North-Easternness' with Tyneside at one extreme, Teesside at the other and Sunderland in between. Only Tyneside has any trace of the double modal construction and it is rare even there. The uncontracted form *cannot* (sometimes pronounced /kanə/, cf. Scots *cannae*) is found in Tyneside and Sunderland, but not Teesside, and negative forms of *do* are distinct in all three varieties, with Tyneside and Sunderland having *divvent* and *dinnet* respectively but Teesside speakers using the more standard *don't*.

Some of the examples cited in this chapter indicate that there are pragmatic constraints on morphosyntactic variation. The young Teessiders in Snell's study demonstrate that the choice between what we might see as 'standard' *me* and 'non-standard' *us* can be manipulated to achieve particular effects in discourse. To arrive at a complete understanding of the nature of morphosyntactic variation in North-Eastern (or any) dialects of English, we need to use a variety of approaches including the analysis of spoken corpora such as NECTE, the collation of elicitation data and the examination of usage in discourse contexts, as in Snell's (2007, 2010) studies. Further features of discourse will be dealt with in the next chapter.

4 Lexis and discourse features

4.1 Introduction: social changes and lexical attrition

The traditional regional vocabulary has been, and continues to be, a very distinctive feature of dialects in the North-East. It includes items which are not used anywhere else in the country and items which reflect the history of the region, from patterns of foreign settlements in the region to its strong connections with agriculture, mining and heavy industry. However, in the course of the twentieth and early twenty-first centuries the North-East, like everywhere else in Britain, experienced considerable social, cultural and technological changes.

Some of these changes have led to increased contact between people from different communities and, as a result, to rapid change in regional dialects. Nowadays, for example, people are a lot more mobile than they were 100 years ago: we often commute relatively long distances to work and, as a result, in the workplace we might encounter people who come from different towns/cities in the region. It is also much easier to visit relatives or friends who live further away. Most families today own a car and/or make regular use of public means of transport (e.g. (inter-)urban buses, trains, planes, and so on). It is easier to stay in regular contact with those who live in other cities, countries and further afield as most of us have access to mobiles, telephones or the internet, all of which we can use for instant messaging, emailing or video-conferencing. While we might take all these facilities for granted, we only need to speak with our parents or grandparents to realise that it was not too long ago that only a few could afford to own a car; that inter-urban telephone calls were expensive and writing letters was the most affordable way of keeping in touch with relatives who lived far away; and that for many families, travelling by train was reserved for holidays. Better means of communication and transport, and increases in geographical and social mobility have favoured frequent and regular contact between speakers of different local varieties, and, as L. Milroy (2002: 7) argues, they have led to a 'large-scale disruption of close-knit, localised networks which have historically maintained highly systematic and complex sets of socially structured linguistic terms'. Thus, many have argued that such disruption of local networks and consequent dialect contact has inevitably resulted in *dialect levelling* – 'the reduction or attrition of *marked* variants' (Trudgill 1986: 98 – italics in original). In this process, localised forms disappear as speakers of different varieties level out differences and converge linguistically (Kerswill 2003). Upton and Widdowson draw a parallel between the widely reported 'weakening and blurring of earlier more localised distinctiveness in regional accents' and the 'erosion of older forms' at the grammatical and lexical levels. They suggest that 'it is at the lexical level . . . that the erosion is seen to have made by far the most significant incursions over the past hundred years' (1999: 10).

Changes to the traditional regional industries (agriculture, coal mining, shipbuilding, steel, and others), particularly in the second half of the twentieth century, have also had a remarkable impact on North-Eastern society and, ultimately, on language use. These industries contributed to the development of very close-knit communities near the coalfields, shipyards, and so on. These groups of people shared working practices, ways of life, cultural values and language that enabled the development of a sense of place and group identity (Townsend and Taylor 1975: 381). The closure of mines and shipyards, the decrease of agricultural practices and the subsequent introduction of new, government-aided, industries and commercial development to battle the increasing unemployment figures resulted in lifestyle changes that would affect local communities across the region and, ultimately, the language of these groups, particularly terms that were used every day in these communities. Other areas of everyday life that are liable to change over time and, therefore, add to the erosion of associated vocabulary are children's games, clothing and fashion.

Simmelbauer (2000), in a study conducted to ascertain the degree of lexical erosion that the traditional dialect lexis of Northumberland had undergone since the mid-1900s, found evidence of lexical attrition in a number of areas. However, dialect words had by no means disappeared overnight. Many, while not being used in everyday conversation, remained, and may still remain, in the passive knowledge of some North-Eastern speakers. As examples of the type of North-Eastern lexis that has fallen out of use we can list terms associated with agricultural and farming activities such as *hemmel* ('cowhouse') and *flaycrow* ('scarecrow'); terms for animals such as *gowk* ('cuckoo'), *ruddick* ('robin redbreast') and *paddock* ('toad'); and clothing terms such as *galluses* ('braces') and *whangs* ('bootlaces, possibly made of leather') (Simmelbauer 2000).

This type of change is inevitable as the vocabulary we use needs to adapt to changes in society: as Wales indicates (2006: 195), 'words must come and go, as in the standard, as new objects, pastimes, etc. appear or disappear, and cultural practices change'.

The rapid loss of English regional/dialect vocabulary across Britain, and in particular in the North-East, has also been aided, as Orton and Wright (1974: 21) argued, by the influence from southern varieties and pressure from standard English:

> [D]ialects in eY [East Yorkshire] have been strongly affected by external pressure from more southerly varieties of English and have already lost, or are losing, characteristic features; Nb [Northumberland] has been penetrated by usages from the North-East, presumably from Scotland, and, as might be expected, St E elements everywhere ousting distinctly regional traits. (Orton and Wright 1974: 21)

As an example, Orton and Wright cite the case of words for 'rivulet' noting that, on a national scale, use of the terms *beck* and *burn* has receded dramatically and been replaced by standard English *stream, brook*. (However, *burn* is still in use in Tyneside and is found in the names of urban waterways such as the *Ouseburn*, which runs through Newcastle.) Orton and Wright further mention the influence of general education and the spread of some technology (e.g. 'wireless programmes' (1974: 21)) as factors that would have contributed to the disappearance of many regional words.

In the remainder of this chapter we look into the North-Eastern dialect lexis in more detail, with a special focus on Tyneside, Wearside and Teesside. First, it is important to establish what research has been conducted into the dialect lexis of the region over the last 125 years. Previous studies constitute an essential body of information which can provide some insight into patterns of lexical use in the region and may help identify evidence of change and/or attrition. This review of previous research is organised chronologically, starting with some of the main compilations of regional dialect vocabulary produced at the end of the nineteenth century, then moving on to the major surveys conducted in the mid-twentieth century (such as the SED), and finally reviewing the most recent surveys. Later, we provide an overview of the various influences on the lexis of the North-East, including Norse, Romani and Celtic languages, before moving on to examine some of the lexical data collected by the authors in the North-East to identify evidence of social and/or geographical variation. The final section in this chapter turns to discourse markers since some of the markers attested in the region differ from those recorded elsewhere in the UK.

4.2 Past research into North-Eastern dialect vocabulary

As Beal argues elsewhere (2010: 73), lexis has been treated as the 'Cinderella' in studies of language variation and change, and this applies equally to research conducted in the North-East. To date, most of our knowledge of the regional dialect vocabulary comes from a few studies conducted up to the 1960s; however, we cannot say that this input has been very extensive. The few studies that in the last 125 years have concerned themselves with producing a lasting account of the vocabulary of the region have focused mostly on traditional rural North-Eastern dialects, especially Northumberland, leaving the dialect lexis of the main three conurbations (Tyneside, Wearside and Teesside) unattended. Thus, this contrasts starkly with the wealth of research conducted into the regional accents and usage of grammar (see Chapters 2 and 3).

In his *Northumberland Words* (1892), Heslop compiled dialect words from the area covered by the old county of Northumberland and the southern bank of the Tyne that used to be part of County Durham (1892: viii).[1] He sometimes includes information on different spellings or on the specific part of the region where particular words were used. Words and expressions commonly used in this region at the time were collected on the spot through many years of observation (1892: xxv). Brockett's *Glossary of North Country Words in Use* (1825) was also one of Heslop's sources, however, and, as a result, some of the terms collected in Heslop's work may have been obsolete by the time of its publication.

Wright's *English Dialect Dictionary* (*EDD*) (1896–1905) and especially Orton and Dieth's *Survey of English Dialects* (SED) (1962–71) are two major landmarks in the development of English dialectology. These traditional studies of English dialect variation have had, and still have, a great influence on contemporary dialect research in England. With a nation-wide scope, they set themselves the objective of recording traditional dialect vocabulary at a time when social changes were occurring rapidly and, thus, constitute 'an exercise in linguistic ecology, dedicated to preserving endangered linguistic species' (Coupland 1992: 5). As a result, these resources have provided us with very valuable information about dialect lexis in the North-East.

Wright's *EDD* (1896–1905) was a large-scale and ambitious project aimed at gathering dialectal vocabulary that was in use in Britain at the time when the study was conducted as well as vocabulary that had been used in the previous 200 years. Wright resorted to glossaries and other sources available at the time in addition to data collected by means of an extensive postal questionnaire of which 12,000 copies were sent around the country. Nevertheless, this source has its downsides, as it does not produce precise information about where a particular entry was recorded (it provides merely the county) (Wakelin 1977: 46–7).

Orton and Dieth's SED, on the other hand, is the only large-scale, nation-wide dialect survey undertaken in the twentieth century. The impact of this survey, developed between 1950 and 1961, was remarkable. It covered phonological, lexical and grammatical differences between rural varieties across England. All the data collected from these English rural communities were recorded in the *Basic Material* (consisting of four volumes with three parts each) and several studies have used this material to map the geographical distribution and frequency of the individual dialect variants elicited (Orton and Wright 1974; Orton et al. 1978; Upton et al. 1987; Upton and Widdowson 1996).

While both the SED and the *EDD* provided us with invaluable records of traditional dialect words used in the North-East between the end of the nineteenth century and the first half of the twentieth century, their findings do not represent the state of dialect vocabulary today. Furthermore, the SED surveyed lexical items that were likely to be used in small rural communities whose way of life was based on mining and/or agriculture and, therefore, its findings are not representative of dialect usage in urban centres. As mentioned at the beginning of this chapter, the increase in social and geographical mobility since the 1950s and 1960s, the disappearance of traditional industries in the North-East and the rapid move of population towards urban areas have inevitably led to changes in vocabulary. Unfortunately, since the SED only a small number of studies have been conducted in the North-East to ascertain the extent to which traditional dialect vocabulary may have experienced change or attrition.

The *Tyneside Linguistic Survey*, conducted in Gateshead around 1969, included a short lexical questionnaire at the end of what was otherwise a fairly free-ranging interview. This was designed to ascertain the participants' knowledge of traditional dialect lexis, but cannot have been one of the researchers' priorities, since the interviewer sometimes failed to administer the questionnaire and sometimes asked about different subsets of the list. Nevertheless, as we shall see in section 4.4.1, these interviews can provide insights into the knowledge and use of local lexis at that time.

Simmelbauer's (2000) study into the *Dialect of Northumberland: A Lexical Investigation*, some of whose findings are discussed above, is the most recent to date and possibly the only one that has aimed to survey a relatively wide area. Its main objective was to investigate Northumbrians' usage and knowledge of a series of dialect words that had been elicited by the SED and the *Linguistic Atlas of Scotland*.

Rather than eliciting traditional dialect lexis, Simmelbauer intended to ascertain whether those items that had been recorded almost fifty years earlier continued being used in the 1990s. For this purpose, she gathered her data from a population sample that consisted not only of elderly speakers but also middle-aged adults and children aged from ten to thirteen, from Newcastle upon Tyne and ten other localities around Northumberland: Cramlington and Blyth in the south-east; Norham, Tweedmouth, Belford, Seahouses and Alnwick in the rural north; Bellingham, Haltwhistle and Hexham in the west. These localities spread across what up to 1974 was the county of Northumberland. However, the inclusion of Newcastle upon Tyne among the surveyed locations indicates an interest in the extent to which dialect lexis has survived in the main conurbation of the North-East. This study contrasts with previous studies of lexis in the region in that: (1) it examines the distribution of the terms surveyed across three generations of speakers; and (2), while it focuses mostly on small towns and villages, it also investigates dialect lexis in a big city.

Simmelbauer's findings provide evidence that many traditional words have been lost in the last few decades and others are now confined to the older generations. Furthermore, as other researchers had argued before (Upton et al. 1994: 23), the findings of this study suggest that lexical erosion has been felt mainly in those semantic fields related to activities that have declined in the last few decades, such as farming (Simmelbauer 2000: 239).

After Simmelbauer's research, the next study we can identify is Burbano-Elizondo's (2001) study of *Lexical Erosion and Lexical Innovation in Tyne and Wear*. Unlike previous lexical research in the North-East, this study focused on two urban centres: Newcastle upon Tyne and Sunderland. Given the absence of research into lexical variation in these two urban centres, Burbano-Elizondo aimed to ascertain the extent to which traditional dialect words that had been attested in the region by some of the previous traditional studies mentioned above (especially the SED) were still used or known at all by adolescents. Furthermore, if some of these traditional dialect words were no longer used or known by adolescents, or if the words were only part of the passive lexical repertoire of the speakers, she intended to ascertain what lexical items had replaced those that had undergone attrition among the young generation. Thus, not only would this study shed some initial light on the extent to which the traditional dialect words recorded in the generation of these teenagers' grandparents a few decades earlier had undergone erosion, but also it would offer an opportunity to compare lexical usage in Sunderland and Newcastle.

Informants were recruited from two secondary schools (one in Sunderland and one in Newcastle upon Tyne) and the findings were compared to Simmelbauer's to determine whether the patterns of attrition identified in some items in Tyne and Wear, mirrored those found in Northumberland. Burbano-Elizondo's findings produced evidence of lexical attrition in a number of traditional dialect words in both groups of informants, for example *gowk* (cuckoo), *cuddy* (donkey), *paddock* (toad or frog), *neb* (nose), *bramble* (blackberry), *bullets* (sweets), *car/cuddy-handed* (left-handed), *skinch* (truce). However, the data also demonstrated that a number of dialect words which had been widely recorded by the SED had stood their ground, at least among teenage urban speakers both in Newcastle and Sunderland, for example *lug* (ear), *gob* (mouth), *tattie* (potato), *hoy* (to throw), *chuck* (to throw), *gadgie* (a bloke or an old man), *bairn* (child), *netty* (toilet).[2] Finally, some lexical items seemed to be almost exclusive to either the Sunderland or the Newcastle informants: for example, *kets* for 'sweets' and *doll off* for 'to play truant' were substantially more frequently elicited from the Sunderland speakers,[3] whereas *wag* for 'to play truant' and *burn* for 'running water smaller than a river' were clearly a lot more widely used by the Newcastle group. Thus, while these findings pointed to the existence of lexical variation between Newcastle and Sunderland and suggested that some traditional dialect words were still known and/or used by adolescents at the turn of the twenty-first century, it was evident that some terms had largely disappeared from the active and passive vocabulary of this generation and been replaced with alternative lexical items. These, however, were not necessarily new local dialect words: often they were standard English words (e.g. *left-handed, sweets, blackberry, potato*) or slang or other terms in general dialect use across large areas of the country (e.g. *spud* for 'potato' or *skive (off)* for 'play truant').

Surprisingly, this exhausts the repertoire of lexical studies in the North-East, particularly in Tyneside, Wearside and Teesside. As can be seen, and as was mentioned at the beginning of this section, studies of lexical variation have not proven popular among the variationist community. This may be partly due to the difficulty of designing methodologies which allow us to record the usage of lexical items in different discourse contexts, since, as Sankoff suggests, 'two different lexical items or structures can almost always have some usages or contexts in which they have different meanings' (1988: 153). In addition to this, although dialectologists often worked on mapping the geographical distribution of dialect words, rarely has lexical variation been used to define geographical or social dialect varieties. Thus, in the limited space of this chapter we begin to redress the absence of lexical research in variationist studies. Corpora of lexical data already exist, collected by Llamas and Burbano-Elizondo in Teesside and Wearside (Llamas 2001a and Burbano-Elizondo 2008, respectively) using the *Survey of Regional English* (SuRE) methodology designed by Llamas (1999, 2001a)[4] – interestingly, no such systematic collection of lexical data has been carried out on Tyneside. Llamas's methodology has been adopted and adapted by many other studies conducted in the UK in the past two decades (Asprey 2007; Finnegan 2011; Pichler 2008; Wallace 2007), but these have tended to focus upon the grammatical and phonological data generated by the methodology, to the detriment of lexical analyses. However, before expanding upon some of the lexical items recorded in the Wearside and Teesside corpora and in some of the studies reviewed in this section, we turn first to a discussion of the sources of the traditional North-Eastern vocabulary.

4.3 Sources of the North-Eastern vocabulary

Wakelin (1972; 1977: 64–5) indicated that one of the main features of English dialect vocabulary is that it is so different from one region to another that even untrained observers are able to spot regional lexical differentiation. He also argued that a high proportion of the traditional English dialectal lexis consists of archaic words which either had been in use more widely across the country (even as part of standard English) in stages of the language as early as Middle English and eventually become dialectal; or had been always confined to specific dialect regions and had never spread beyond them. The former is certainly the case for many traditional dialect words that survive today, or have survived until recently, in the North-East of England. For example, the word *burn* ('a rivulet or a stream') is a native/Anglo-Saxon word (OE *burna*) that is obsolete in standard English and that the *OED* defines as dialectal (mainly northern). This term can be found in the name of many rivers and towns/villages in the North-East (for example *North Bitchburn, Otterburn, Burnhope* and the *Ouseburn*, which runs through the city of Newcastle). The SED recorded it only in Northumberland, but previous sources like the *EDD* placed it in Yorkshire, Durham and Cumbria too, which may suggest that its distribution area has receded since the late nineteenth century.

Old English (native) vocabulary, like the term just discussed, constitutes an important part of the traditional dialect vocabulary of the North-East, especially since in Anglo-Saxon times the North-East region was part of the Anglian kingdom of Northumbria. Thus, language differences between this region and more southerly ones would have already existed at that time. Many of the regional dialect words which derive from Old English and which the SED recorded as being still in use in the North-East in the 1950s bear a connection with rural and everyday life. Some examples include words that by no means were exclusive to the North-East (for example *brambles* ('blackberries'), recorded in Northumberland, Durham, large areas of West Yorkshire and Lincolnshire by the SED) and others, like *burn* (see above), which by the time of the SED would have been more specific to the North-East, particularly to Northumberland.[5]

Further dialect words that derive from Old English include *bairn* (from OE *baern*, 'child') which the SED recorded in the far north, Yorkshire and Lincolnshire, and the *OED* today associates with northern England and Scotland but argues that, at some point, it would have been used in the south of England since its use is attested in Shakespeare's *Winter's Tale*. It continues to be used today in areas of northern England and Scotland. *Wag* (OE *wagian*, 'to play truant') was recorded by the *EDD* in Northumberland, yet the *OED* defines it as slang.

According to Simmelbauer (2000: 21), dialect words which descend from Old English sources are a lot more numerous in what used to be the old county of Northumberland than in County Durham and dialects further south (such as Teesside). This is not because the territories that today we know as County Durham had a particularly high number of Scandinavian settlements as a result of the Viking invasion towards the end of the Old English period. In fact, the northern edge of the Scandinavian Belt (the name by which we refer to the territories that were most heavily settled by the Scandinavians towards the end of the Old English period) stretches from Cumbria, in the north-western corner of England, across diagonally to the eastern coast of south Durham and the Teesdale valley; and its southern limits run diagonally across the country from the areas around the mouth of the River Mersey to approximately the mouth of the Thames. While verging on the Scandinavian Belt, County Durham was outside this region. Yet, its geographical proximity makes it likely that elements of the Scandinavian language would have spread northwards into the current County of Durham as a result of contact between the northern European settlers and the native English speakers. Furthermore, as we saw in section 1.3.1, the distribution of place names, in particular, gives us an idea of the patterns of Scandinavian settlement around north-eastern England: many more place names with Old Norse elements can be found in and around southern Durham (a few around the Wear), Teesside and north Yorkshire than in Northumberland, Tyne and Wear and northern Durham, where the Scandinavian influence was small (Wakelin 1977: 19). Scandinavian place names around Teesside and south Durham mostly contain the ON elements -*by* ('farm' or 'town') and -*thorpe* ('village') (for example *Aislaby, Cleasby, Killerby, Ormesby, Thornaby on Tees, Yearby, Middlethorpe Pinchinthorpe, Thorpe Thewles, Linthorpe,* etc.), but we can also find place names with other ON elements, such as *Boosbeck* which contains the ON word *beck* meaning 'stream', and *Hunderthwaite* which contains -*thwaite* meaning 'an isolated piece of land' (Baugh and Cable 1993: 96; Institute for Name-Studies 2010).

The Scandinavian people left considerable traces of their settlement on the English language and, in particular, on its vocabulary. Some of the words that were borrowed from their language are still in use today both in standard English and in regional dialects of the Danelaw. Many loanwords, with time, found their way into standard English, for example *egg, husband, kid, get, give, sky, take* and *window.* Furthermore, even some of the pronouns used today originate from Scandinavian, for example *they, their, them,* which gives us an idea of the extent to which this language contact situation influenced English. The contact between the Scandinavians and the native English also left many words in the regional dialects of the Danelaw, many of which have survived in modern regional varieties. In the North-East, for example, many dialect words of Scandinavian origin were recorded by the SED in County Durham and the localities around Teesside, though not in Northumberland (Orton and Wright 1974). *Beck* (ON *bekkr,* 'a stream or rivulet') was recorded in an area that mirrored the Scandinavian Belt, including Durham and the Teesside area but excluding Northumberland, which appeared as the relic area for the OE term *burn* (see above) alongside Wearside and north-west Cumbria. As for *beck,* the distribution shown by the SED for *lake* (ON *leika,* 'to play') and *slape* (ON *sleipr,* 'slippery') reflected the Scandinavian Belt, thus including Durham and the localities around Teesside. Yet, neither of them was attested in the areas surveyed around Tyneside, Wearside and Northumberland. In the SED data, *ket* (ON *kjot,* 'rubbish') was confined to areas of south County Durham, including areas around Teesside. Interestingly, however, both Burbano-Elizondo (2001) and Simmelbauer (2000) attested the use of this word in Sunderland and west Northumberland, respectively, to refer to 'sweets'. In both studies, though, this term was only sporadically recorded in Tyneside.

Other dialect words of Scandinavian origin have been attested not only in Durham and Teesside but also around Northumberland, Tyneside and Wearside. However, these are a lot less numerous. Such is the case with *loup* (ON *hloupa,* 'jump'), which was attested around the whole of the North-East, Cumberland, Lancashire and north Yorkshire in the SED (Orton and Wright 1974: M57). More recently, this word has been attested in Northumberland (Simmelbauer 2000: 119–20) and to some extent in Sunderland (Burbano-Elizondo 2001). *Bait* (ON *beita*), meaning 'packed lunch', was already recorded by the *EDD* in Northumberland and Durham and other northern counties. Simmelbauer (2000: 137–8) confirms the survival of this lexical item among all generations in both Northumberland and Newcastle upon Tyne at the end of the twentieth century. Burbano-Elizondo (2008) also recorded this word in Sunderland as a variant for 'food taken to work'.

So far we have seen some of the major foreign influences on the dialect lexis of the North-East. However, another source of influence that needs to be mentioned is that of Romani, a language which originated in north-western India (Baugh and Cable 1993: 22). It was brought to the British Isles by immigrants from eastern and central Europe (from Russia, Poland and Bosnia, as well as other areas) as early as the sixteenth century. On arrival, these minority language speakers, often known as 'Gipsies' (especially in their countries of origin) settled across the country. Matras (2007) indicates that, although Romani was the native language of these travelling communities, progressively descendants of the original migrants adopted English. However, they continued using a lot of Romani vocabulary when speaking English, and consequently this English dialect is generally known as Angloromani (Matras 2007).

Contact between British Romani communities and local British communities must have led to the gradual incorporation of a number of Romani words into English. Beal (2010) argues that this source of foreign influence tends to be neglected in traditional dialect research, suggesting that this may be due to the fact that its effects have been felt most strongly on urban varieties or maybe because, in the absence of any definite pattern of geographical distribution, Romani words are usually regarded as slang. Generally, words originating from this source can be identified in the dialects of areas which were on the travelling routes of the Romani travellers or in the dialects of areas where traditional markets and fairs took place (Beal 2010: 61). Thus, some dialects in the North-East are among those where the Romani influence is identifiable. According to Matras (2007), the Scottish–English border was one of those areas that attracted Romani settlers and, as a result, he argues, Romani words have been assimilated into many local dialects in Northumberland. Among these borrowings we find *gadgie*, meaning 'a bloke or an old man'. This term, which comes from the Romani *gaujo*, used to refer to 'a white man, a non-Romany', is still widely known in Northumberland, Tyneside and Wearside (Beal 2010; Burbano-Elizondo 2001: 64; Simmelbauer 2000). *Charver*, from Romani *čhavo* (meaning 'unmarried Romani male' or 'male Romani child'), is defined by the *OED* as an English regional (slang) term, specifically associated with the North-East, which is used to refer to '[a] young person of a type characterised by brash and loutish behaviour and the wearing of designer-style clothes (esp. sportswear); usually with connotations of a low social status'. This regional term contrasts with the much more widespread use of *chav* which derives from the same Romani word (*čhavo*) and has the same meaning as *charver*, and which the *OED* defines as a derogatory slang term (originally from the south of England) used in the UK. Two further examples that Simmelbauer argues are recognised as 'gipsywords' by the older generations in the North-East are *moat* ('woman') and *barrey* ('good-looking') (2000: 18).

The final source of influence on the North-Eastern dialect vocabulary to be discussed in this section is the Celtic element. Orton and Wright (1974: 32) indicate that some of the very few words of Celtic origin that have survived in regional dialects are found generally in areas bordering Wales and down into Cornwall. Some, though, have been attested in Northumberland where they might have spread from Scotland. The infiltration of Gaelic/Celtic words into Northumbrian dialects is not surprising given the proximity of this region to Scotland and the migration of both Scottish and Irish workers to the North-East in search of employment in the coal mines in the eighteenth and nineteenth centuries as a result of the increasing industrialisation of the area at the time.

Some examples of words of Celtic origin in traditional North-Eastern dialects include: *car-handed*, *brock* and *gob*. *Car-handed*, meaning 'left-handed', derived from the Celtic *cearr*, used to mean 'wrong, awkward' (*OED*). The evidence available from the SED seems to suggest that this term was confined to northern Northumberland in the mid-twentieth century, yet, no evidence of it was found either in Newcastle or Sunderland young speakers by Burbano-Elizondo (2001). *Brock*, used to mean 'a badger', from Celtic *broc*, was found, according to the *EDD*, in all northern counties and Scotland. However, the SED recorded it only in four Northumberland localities, which suggests that, at the time, this word was receding. By the time Simmelbauer conducted her study in Northumberland, she found that only a few of her informants were familiar with *brock* and she argued that it seemed that active usage of this word was giving way to passive knowledge (2000: 69). Finally, *gob* ('mouth') is by no means confined to the North-East. This term is defined in the *OED* as a northern dialect word/slang of obscure origin. However, it is suggested that it possibly originates from Gaelic and Irish *gob*, also used to refer to the mouth. The SED, which also refers to the obscure origin of this word, attested it in a wide geographical area consisting of southern Northumberland, Durham, Westmorland, Cumberland, Lancashire and areas of Yorkshire, Derbyshire, Lincolnshire and Norfolk. Although the *OED* makes reference to the widespread usage of this term in northern dialects today, *gob* was also frequently elicited by Simmelbauer (2000: 95) in most of the localities she surveyed in Northumberland (including Newcastle) and by Burbano-Elizondo (2001: 84), both in Newcastle and Sunderland.[6]

As we have seen in this section, the make-up of the traditional North-Eastern vocabulary reflects rather closely the patterns of contact that have taken place in the region. All these social movements have made of the regional lexis a distinctive feature of the dialects of the North-East, both rich and diverse. Furthermore, many of the words we have discussed so far in this chapter demonstrate that, as we argued at the beginning of this chapter, dialect vocabulary is in constant flux and changes to adapt to times and society. The examples given provide us not only with evidence of dialect words that entered these varieties centuries ago and still continue being used, but also with words that, after having been in regular use in the region for centuries, are undergoing, or have undergone, lexical attrition. This loss of regional vocabulary, however, does not necessarily mean that dialect lexis in the North-East, or elsewhere, is decreasing. As a result of the constant process of change to which language is subjected, as some words may fall out of use, others are incorporated into the speaker's repertoire, either to replace the ones that have disappeared or to refer to new notions that may have appeared as a consequence of social change or new inventions. The following section turns to explore in more depth some of the lexical data collected by the authors in order to discuss any evidence of lexical innovation and social variation in the dialects of Tyneside, Wearside and Teesside.

4.4 Case studies

4.4.1 *Case study 1:* The Tyneside Linguistic Survey *lexical questionnaire*

As discussed above, some of the interviews conducted for the *Tyneside Linguistic Survey* (TLS) included a lexical questionnaire designed to ascertain the extent of participants' knowledge/use of a number of 'local' words. The collection of such data seems not to have been a priority for the TLS team: the questionnaire was administered to only

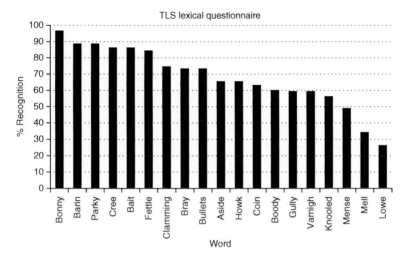

Figure 4.1 Recognition rates for words in the TLS lexical questionnaire

fifty of the participants whose interviews survive, and the interviewer very rarely completed the questionnaire. At times, he revealed a negative attitude to this part of the interview with remarks such as 'this is boring' or 'it's obvious you're going to say the same to all of these so we'll skip them'. Nevertheless, some generalisations can be drawn from these data, and there are some useful qualitative data to be extracted from the answers (Figure 4.1). The interviewer would introduce this questionnaire as follows:

> I've got a list of words here which are all fairly local sort of Tyneside words. I would just like to know, for each one, firstly if you're familiar with it you-know . . . and secondly, if you ever use it yourself.

The full list of words is: *aside* (for SE *beside*), *bairn, bait* (= 'packed lunch'), *beck*,[7] *bonny, boody, bray* (= 'hit'), *bullets* (= 'sweets'), *clamming, clarts, coin* (= 'turn a corner'), *cree, dunch, fettle, gully* (= 'bread knife'), *howk, hoy, ken, kep, knooled, lowe, mell, mense, nebber, parky, poorly, stot* and *varnigh*. Of these, *beck, clarts, dunch, hoy, kep, ket, nebber, poorly* and *stot* were presented to less than half of the forty-nine participants who were given the questionnaire, so we have excluded these from our analysis. In Figure 4.1 we have assigned a score of 2 where the participant both knew and claimed to use the word, 1 where the participant knew it but denied using it and 0 where the participant neither knew nor used the word. Since hardly any of the participants were presented even with all the words included here, we present the results as percentages of possible scores. Thus, if a word was presented to all forty-nine participants and all forty-nine both knew and used it, the score would be 98, or 100 per cent, but if a word was presented to only forty participants, then the maximum possible score would be 80. Figure 4.1 shows the results by word.

Where a word scores over 70 per cent, as is the case with *bonny, bairn, parky, cree, bait, fettle, clamming, bray* and *bullets*, this indicates that it was both known and used fairly widely. Words scoring between 50 and 70 per cent were widely known, but not so widely used, and those scoring under 50 per cent were neither known to nor used by the majority of participants. The former category includes *aside, howk, coin, boody, varnigh* and *knooled* and the latter *mense* in the expression *be more to your mense* (= 'get on with it), *mell* (= 'a large hammer') and *lowe* (= 'light'). Several participants who claimed to know but not use certain words remarked that their parents would have used them, or that they themselves would have used them when younger. In other cases, the participant expressed an opinion about the word: several dispute the inclusion of *cree* as a local word, claiming that this is simply the standard word for a pigeon's living quarters, and others object to the word *bray*, perhaps because of the violent action referred to (*'I'll bray ye!'* would be a threat to hit someone).

There was also some correlation between the social class of participants and their knowledge of these words. Of the participants with individual scores between 70 per cent and 100 per cent, nineteen out of twenty were working class; all those with scores below 50 per cent were middle class and of those with scores between 50 per cent and 70 per cent, ten were middle class and fourteen were working class. So we can conclude that all the working-class participants knew and/or used the majority of the words, though the scores for middle-class participants ranged from a very low 25 per cent to 73 per cent. There was no correlation between these scores and the age or gender of participants, so we are not able to draw any conclusions about lexical attrition from these data: indeed, several participants claimed to have heard children using words that they no longer used themselves as adults.

4.4.2 Case study 2: Lads and lasses

The words *lad* and *lass* are associated with Tyneside at least partly as a result of their appearance in the chorus of the 'Geordie National Anthem', *The Blaydon Races*.

Oh me lads, you should've seen us gannin'
Passing the folks along the road

just as they were stannin'
Aal the lads and lasses there
aal wi' smilin' faces
Gannin' along the Scotswood Road
To see the Blaydon Races[8]

Beat Glauser analysed the geographical distribution of lexical variants in the semantic fields BOYS/GIRLS; SONS/DAUGHTERS in SED material. While acknowledging that the analysis of semantic fields in data from dialect surveys is problematic because 'the members of a semantic field cannot be collected exhaustively unless they are known beforehand' (1985: 37), he noted:

- a clear isogloss reflecting the 'North-South' divide, whereby LAD is used almost exclusively north of a line running from southern Shropshire to the Wash;
- a more complex picture with regard to LASS, since there are more variants involved, but LASS still mainly confined to the North;
- a wider currency for LAD than LASS, with combinations of LAD/GIRL much more common than LASS/BOY.

He concluded that 'the boundaries in question are the result of social, systematical, variational and geographical forces' and suggested that 'we should now check with linguistic reality thirty years later' (Glauser 1985: 55).

Beal and Burbano-Elizondo (2010) took up Glauser's challenge by analysing data from (1) the *Phonological Variation and Change* (PVC) project, collected in Newcastle in 1994 and incorporated into NECTE, and (2) that collected by Burbano-Elizondo in Sunderland between 2003 and 2005. The PVC data consist of transcriptions of dyadic conversations, while the Sunderland data were collected using the SuRE methodology, so the two datasets were analysed separately.

Glauser was dealing with data from a nationwide survey in which data were elicited systematically using the same questions in every locality, and so was able to plot the distribution of variants systematically. In the case of the Newcastle data, it would be futile to simply count the tokens of LAD and LASS because these would not occur at a consistent rate in free conversation. Instead, Beal and Burbano-Elizondo compared the use of LAD and LASS with that of their standard English synonyms BOY and GIRL, respectively. In Figure 4.2, the bars represent the proportion of LAD vs BOY and LASS vs GIRL by speakers grouped according to age and gender.[9]

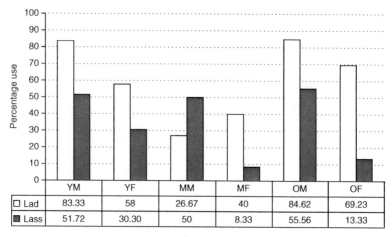

	YM	YF	MM	MF	OM	OF
☐ Lad	83.33	58	26.67	40	84.62	69.23
■ Lass	51.72	30.30	50	8.33	55.56	13.33

Speaker groups

Figure 4.2 Proportions of LAD (vs BOY) and LASS (vs GIRL) in PVC data.

Figure 4.2 shows that every group except the middle-aged males uses LAD for 'boy' more than LASS for 'girl', but that LASS has not fallen out of use. Moreover, the group with the second highest proportional use of LASS is the young males, so it would appear that LASS is not declining. So, with regard to the Newcastle data, the answer to Glauser's first question is yes, LAD is at least proportionally more widespread than LASS. There is no clear pattern according to age, except that the middle-aged group use both words less, possibly a classic example of age-grading. With the exception of the middle-aged speakers, males use both LAD and LASS more than females of the same age group do, so there appears to be variation according to gender. What complicates the picture here, compared with that from the SED data, is that both LAD and LASS can be used with a much wider range of referents than just 'son' or 'daughter', so they contrast with a number of other terms as well as BOY and GIRL.

Figure 4.3 shows all instances of LAD/BOY in the major senses in which they co-vary; meaning 'son', 'young man' and 'sexual partner'. In the case of 'son', both also co-vary with the word SON itself, and in the case of 'sexual partner', the word HUSBAND is also used. Here we can see that LAD for 'son' is only used once; for 'partner' it is more common than BOYFRIEND, but less common than HUSBAND. However, the vast majority of uses of LAD are with the meaning 'young man'. Where older males are referred to, MAN and BLOKE are the most common words.

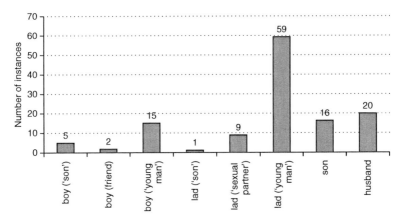

Figure 4.3 Instances of LAD and BOY and synonyms in PVC data

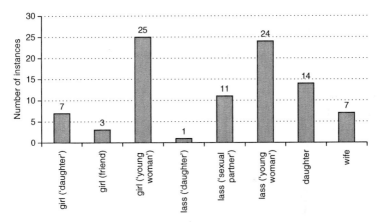

Figure 4.4 Instances of LASS and GIRL and synonyms in PVC data.

Figure 4.4 shows the distribution of LASS and its various synonyms in the PVC data. The distribution of LASS across semantic categories is similar to that of LAD, with 'young woman' being the most frequent. In this case, though, GIRL is a much stronger rival than BOY was for LAD. LASS for 'daughter' is as rare as LAD for 'son', and the proportion of LASS to GIRLFRIEND for 'sexual partner' is similar to that of LAD to BOYFRIEND. However, LASS is also used for 'wife', whereas LAD for 'husband' is rare.

Figures 4.5 and 4.6 show variation according to social class in the usage of younger and older PVC participants, respectively. Figure 4.5 shows that, among the younger speakers, middle-class subjects use both

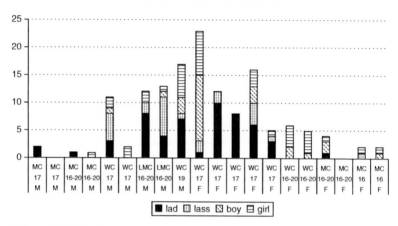

Figure 4.5 Variation in use of LAD and LASS vs BOY and GIRL according to class and gender (younger participants)

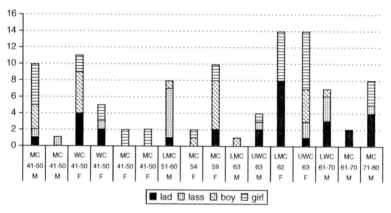

Figure 4.6 Variation in use of LAD and LASS vs BOY and GIRL according to class and gender (older participants).

LAD and LASS less frequently than their working- and lower-middle-class peers. The exceptions here are the two working-class females who never use LAD or LASS. This dyad is atypical in that it is made up of two young British Pakistani women, who use GIRL and BOY exclusively to refer to their peers. In fact, the middle-class speakers use few tokens of any of these words, which could simply be a consequence of their topics of conversation. Apart from the two British Pakistani women though, all the young working-class speakers use either LAD or LASS. Among the older speakers, as we can see from Figure 4.6, it is also the case that all the working-class speakers use either LAD or LASS, but other than this no clear patterns emerge with regard to variation according to class.

Apart from a greater tendency for working-class and lower-middle-class speakers to use LAD and LASS, there seems to be no correlation between social class and variable use of these words. This is illustrated clearly in the case of one lower-middle-class dyad, one of whom consistently refers to his partner as 'wor lass', while the other uses 'the/my girlfriend'. Examples of this usage are:

Wor lass was drinking purple passions all night. (PVC 1a)

Got to go over to the girlfriend's concert first though. (PVC 1b)

These two young men are friends, matched in terms of age and class. This variation suggests that use of LAD/LASS may well be a matter of style and/or stance rather than sociolect.

The data from Burbano-Elizondo's study of Sunderland are more similar to SED data in so far as they consist of responses to a questionnaire rather than tokens occurring in conversation. However, the SuRE questionnaire is very different from that administered by the SED (see Figure 4.7). It elicits multiple words for each notion, as subjects are asked to write down all the words they use and are given at least a week to do this rather than being limited to the first words they think of. Notions are arranged into Sense Relation Networks (SRNs). As we see in the figure, each SRN groups notions into semantic fields, which, in turn, are also interconnected. This 'web of words' format also encourages subjects to think about the relationships within and between semantic fields. The words we are considering in this chapter were elicited from the 'relations and relationships' section of the PEOPLE SRN, shown as Figure 4.7. LAD and LASS were elicited under 'partner', 'child' and 'brother/sister' and in every case a range of synonyms was elicited. For 'brother/sister', LAD and LASS were elicited from just one female and two male subjects, all over fifty years of age in the case of LAD; one of the males between thirty-one and fifty years of age and one male and one female over fifty in the case of LASS. For 'boy/girl' and 'sexual partner', there was more widespread use of LAD and LASS. Burbano-Elizondo found that for words elicited under 'male/female child', male respondents only gave LAD/LASS, whereas females gave BOY/SON and GIRL/DAUGHTER as well. The widest range of variants was elicited for 'partner'. For female respondents, BOYFRIEND and HUSBAND were most frequent, but LAD, always preceded by 'my' or 'our', was elicited from five females and two males. In the sense of 'female partner', LASS

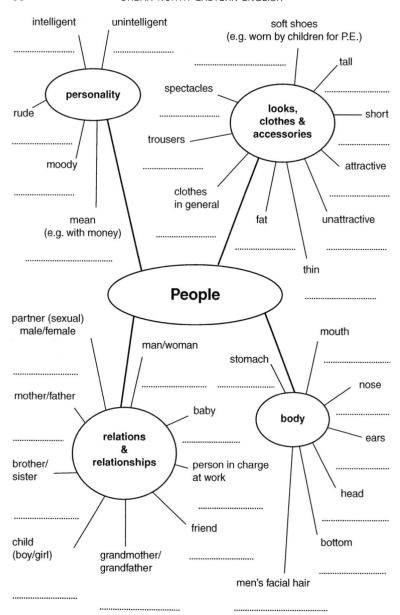

Figure 4.7 'People' sense relation network (SRN)

was elicited more frequently than any other term, from both male and female subjects. As with LAD, LASS was always preceded by 'my' or 'our/ wor'. It is interesting that LASS is elicited more frequently than LAD in the sense 'sexual partner', and this from both male and female subjects. This is contrary to Glauser's finding that LAD was more widely used than LASS, but, of course, he was only looking at responses to questions designed to elicit words for 'boy/girl' and 'son/ daughter'. In fact, LAD and LASS were not found as responses to SED questions designed to elicit words for 'husband' and 'wife'.

The conclusions to be drawn from Beal and Burbano-Elizondo's analysis are that neither LAD nor LASS shows any sign of disappearing from usage in Newcastle or Sunderland, but that, in accordance with Glauser's findings, LAD is used more than LASS with the meanings 'boy/girl', 'son/daughter' and 'young man/ woman'. However, Beal and Burbano-Elizondo's study shows that LASS is used more than LAD in the sense 'sexual partner', and that it is mainly in this sense that LASS continues to be used.

4.5 Discourse markers

There are a number of discourse markers that are characteristic of North-Eastern dialects and that have been attested in data collected in Tyneside, Wearside and Teesside.

4.5.1 Intensifiers

The first type of discourse marker we discuss here is intensifiers. In some North-Eastern varieties, the intensifier *geet* is used, as in the example:

This is geet hard, Sir. (Beal 1993: 210)

Beal (1993) argued that *geet* was 'possibly unique to Tyneside'; however, this intensifier was widely recognised by Burbano-Elizondo's (2008) Sunderland informants who argued that *geet* would be used in Sunderland. They nonetheless indicated that in Sunderland this intensifier would not be realised as *geet* but *git* instead. Beal (1993: 210) also suggested that a potential etymology for *geet* is the Scots intensifier *gey*, a French loanword, arguing that in Tyneside the Scots form would be realised with a monophthong /i:/ to which 'an underlying /t/ may have been added by inference' possibly as a result of the frequent presence of glottalisation of final /t/ in word-final position in the Tyneside accent.

Of course, *geet* is not the only intensifier used in the North-East: in fact it is relatively rare. Barnfield and Buchstaller (2010) carried out a 'real-time' analysis of variation and change in intensifiers in Tyneside English, comparing data from the TLS and PVC subsets of the NECTE corpus with data collected between 2007 and 2008 for the NECTE2 corpus.[10] They found that, in the sample they analysed from the TLS part of NECTE, the most frequently used intensifier was *very*, while in the PVC sample, *very* was much less frequent, with *dead* and *really* proving most popular. That this represents an ongoing trend is suggested by the fact that it is the younger speakers in the PVC who favoured *dead* and *really*. The NECTE2 data indicated that *dead* was no longer the most popular choice: *very* and *really* were competing for the 'top spot', with a number of innovative variants appearing at lower frequencies. Among the latter were *pure* and *canny*: the former also appearing in studies of urban Scots (Macaulay 2006), but *canny* exclusive to the North-East of England. This use of *canny* as an intensifier is captured in Jonathan Tulloch's novel *The Season Ticket*, which is set in Gateshead: 'That's yer talent. Canny strong an' all' (Tulloch 2000: 11).

4.5.2 *Sentence-final elements*

There are also a number of sentence-final features that are characteristic of North-Eastern dialects. *But*, for example, may be used in sentence-final position to mean 'though' (e.g. *I'll manage but*),[11] in addition to its standard usage as a conjunction. Such use of *but* has been attested not only in Tyneside (Beal 1993: 211) but also in Wearside. In the latter, although Burbano-Elizondo's (2008) informants argued that such a feature is more typical of Tyneside English, there were a number of instances in which the speakers themselves used this non-standard feature. Examples were:

> *[They are] expressions I tend to use but.* (MM29)

> *I don't do that anymore but.* (MM14)

Like may also be found in sentence-final position in North-Eastern dialects. Although this focusing device may be found in other positions, Beal (2008: 136) indicates that its discourse function at the end of a sentence or clause is to add emphasis. Examples of usage of sentence-final *like* may be found in the corpora from Tyneside, Wearside and Teesside:

That's the first time I've heard that like. (OM07)

Kids would say that like. (YF09)

I'm a Geordie, me, like. (NECTE)

4.5.3 Other uses of like

While North-Eastern dialects share this traditional use of *like* with Scottish English, as in many other English varieties worldwide, North-Eastern speakers may also use *like* in the middle of a sentence/clause, where it adopts an explanatory function (Beal 2008: 136), as in:

Now I think [the word] 'loo' is more for like women. (OF08)

Finally, North-Eastern speakers, especially those in the younger generations, have also adopted the use of *like* as a quotative: a feature that in recent years has spread widely across the English-speaking world. Beal and Corrigan (2011) note that, while speakers from the TLS subsection of NECTE almost always use *say* to introduce quotes, the younger speakers in the PVC subsection (aged seventeen to twenty in 1994) use a variety of quotatives, including *go* and *be like*, as in the following example:

*Everyone thinks it's dead strange. Sitting at dancing, and everyone's **going** 'Oh Emma, who are you going on holiday with?' and she's **going** 'Her boyfriend' and they **were like** 'Your . . . best friend's going on holiday with your boyfriend?'* (PVC, female, middle class, age seventeen)

4.5.4 Right dislocation

Repetition of the grammatical subject at the end of a sentence, known as right dislocation, is a discourse feature used throughout the North-East. Examples from Tyneside, Wearside and Teesside are:

I'm a Geordie, me, like. (NECTE)

That's awful that! (OF08)

He's lush him. (OF08)

She's a liar, her. (Moore and Snell 2011: 13)

Right dislocation is by no means exclusive to dialects of the North-East of England. Moore and Snell (2011) demonstrate that younger working-class speakers in both Bolton and Teesside use right-dislocated pronouns to carry out 'social work'. Examples from the Teesside data, which were collected from primary schoolchildren aged between eight and ten, are:

She's a liar her. I hate her. (Moore and Snell 2011: 13)

God, you're gay, you. (Moore and Snell 2011: 15)

Give us that lid, you. (Moore and Snell 2011: 13)

According to Moore and Snell, in the first of these examples, the speaker is using right dislocation 'to negatively evaluate' the girl referred to, but also to 'draw the others into alliance' with the speaker. In the second example, what appears an aggressive statement out of context is explained as emphasising the 'close bond of solidarity' between close male friends, while the third is one of several instances of right dislocation in imperatives, 'the most direct and potentially risky form of directives' (Moore and Snell 2011: 15). Moore and Snell point out that all the instances of second-person tags in the Teesside data and the vast majority of those in the Bolton data, occurred in the conversations of working-class speakers. It would appear that, at least within the north of England, right-dislocated pronouns are widely used by working-class speakers to position speakers and addressees within the social group rather than as markers of regional identity.

4.5.5 Terms of endearment

Terms of endearment are also important elements in the organisation of discourse as they mark the relationship that exists between the speaker and the hearer, or may be used to gain someone's attention There are a number of terms of endearment which are characteristic of (yet not always exclusive to) North-Eastern dialects. These can be heard in a number of different situations, which range from interactions between friends and family members to interactions between total strangers in the street or service encounters.

Love is a term of endearment which, although widely used in the North-East, is not exclusive to this region: it can be heard in many other northern dialects, such as Yorkshire, Liverpool and Lancashire. This form of address may be used to show familiarity or often speakers may use it to address total strangers in service encounters. Generally, this term is used more frequently by older speakers addressing younger speakers, or in male–female, female–male or female–female interactions (Beal 2008: 400). Its usage may certainly lead to misunderstandings and confusion if used to address, for example, non-native speakers who may not be familiar with the subtleties of this word. A personal anecdote might explain this: a few years ago, when one of the authors was living in Sunderland, she remembers that one of her Austrian male work colleagues became very confused after a woman who was a lot older than him addressed him in the street using *love* since, he argued, he did not know the woman, let alone love her!

More specific to the North-East is the term *pet*, which may be used in female–female, male–female or female–male interactions, either by people who are familiar with one another or by total strangers. Also typical of the North-East is the use of *bonny lad* and *son* which, Beal (2008: 400) explains, are terms which are equivalent to the more widely spread term *mate* and may be used between males of the same age. *Mate* itself, however, is also in use in North-Eastern dialects to address informally men (and possibly women), whether known or not to the speaker. Thus, its function may not just be that of addressing individuals the speaker is friends with but also gaining someone's attention.

Last but not least, in the North-East *man* may be used to address either males and/or females in the same way as US *guys* and may express annoyance or impatience (Beal 2008: 400). The following example from the *Tyneside Linguistic Survey* involves a participant responding to the interviewer's question about where she goes for holidays:

I divvent gan on holidays, man.

The implication is that the question was ridiculous, since holidays are a luxury she cannot afford.

4.6 Conclusion

We have seen in this chapter that, while some lexical items traditionally associated with the North-East of England are now unknown to younger speakers, others continue to be used in everyday discourse. The dialects of Tyneside and Wearside tend to have more regional vocabulary in common than either of these does with Teesside, where the influence of the Danelaw is more apparent. Although the case studies in 4.5 demonstrate that variation and change in the lexicon is an area worth investigating, there is a need for much more research. The new *Diachronic Electronic Corpus of Tyneside English* (DECTE) currently under development will provide up-to-date and accessible material for such studies, at least as far as Tyneside is concerned.

Notes

1. The subtitle of this glossary is 'a glossary of words used in the county of Northumberland and on the Tyneside'.

2. Note that while some of these words exist in general dialect use today (e.g. *gob*, *chuck*), others have traditionally been part of the lexicon of the northern, or more specifically North-Eastern, dialects, e.g. *lug, hoy, gadgie, bairn, netty*.

3. No previous surveys in the region had recorded either of these two lexical items.

4. This methodology introduced an innovatory data-collection method which enabled the collection of phonological, grammatical *and* lexical data quickly and easily. Its aim was to facilitate the recording of informal speech from speakers so that researchers could undertake 'multi-levelled analyses of both regionally and socially comparable data' (Llamas 1999: 97–8).

5. This, like a number of words found within England only or mainly in Northumberland, is also in widespread use in Scotland.

6. Note that *gob* was also frequently elicited by Burbano-Elizondo in the data she collected for her study of the Sunderland language and identity (2008).

7. However, it is interesting to note that a minority of participants did claim to know and use *beck*. This accords with the distribution found in SED data, where *beck* was attested in Washington, which, like Gateshead in 1969, is in the far north of County Durham.

8. See Beal (2000) and Hermeston (2011) for discussion of the iconicity of this song.

9. YM = young males, YF = young females; MM = middle-aged males, MF = middle-aged females, OM = older males, OF = older females. (The young, middle and older age groups are 16–30, 50–60; and over 60 respectively.)

10. The NECTE and NECTE2 corpora are currently being amalgamated into a new *Diachronic Electronic Corpus of Tyneside English* (DECTE). See http://research.ncl.ac.uk/decte/

11. Example from Pellowe et al. (1972: 42).

5 Annotated bibliography and references

5.1 History, geography, demography and culture

- Chase, M. (1995), 'The Teesside Irish in the nineteenth century', *Cleveland History: The Bulletin of the Cleveland and Teesside Local History Society*, 69: 3–23.
  This paper deals with the growing numbers of Irish-born migrants to Middlesbrough during the nineteenth century and focuses on their practices and assimilation.
- Colls, Robert and Bill Lancaster (eds) (2001), *Newcastle upon Tyne: A Modern History*, Chichester: L. Phillimore.
  This is a collection of chapters on various aspects of the social and economic history of Newcastle in the nineteenth and twentieth centuries.
- Dodds, Glen L. (2001), *A History of Sunderland*, 2nd edition, Sunderland: Albion Press.
  This book provides a comprehensive history of Wearside from the first settlements in the area to the end of the twentieth century. It guides the reader through the defining events that have given Sunderland its characteristic identity.
- Green, Adrian and A. J. Pollard (eds) (2007), *Regional Identities in North-East England, 1300–2000*, Woodbridge: Boydell.
  This is a collection of chapters by scholars involved with the Arts and Humanities Research Council-funded Centre for North East England History, exploring aspects of regional identity in the North-East from medieval to modern times.
- Lewis, R. and D. Ward (1995), 'Culture, politics and assimilation: the Welsh on Teesside, c. 1850–1940', *Welsh History Review*, 17.4: 550–70.
  This paper focuses specifically on Welsh migration to Middlesbrough during the growth of the industrial urban centre.
- Pollard, A. J. (ed.), *Middlesbrough Town and Community, 1830–1950*, Stroud: Sutton Publishing.

This is a collection of chapters on various aspects of the social, political and cultural history of Middlesbrough from the nineteenth to the mid-twentieth century.

5.2 Phonetics and phonology

- Atkinson, John (2011), 'Linguistic variation and change in a North-East border town: a sociolinguistic study of Darlington', PhD thesis, Newcastle University.
  This doctoral dissertation reports a quantitative study of phonological variation and change in progress in Darlington.
- Burbano-Elizondo, Lourdes (2008), 'Language variation and identity in Sunderland', PhD thesis, University of Sheffield.
  This doctoral dissertation reports a study of language variation and identity conducted in Sunderland. The accent variables analysed here were selected by exploring the informants' perceptions of linguistic difference, with the intention of ascertaining whether their awareness of variation between Sunderland and Newcastle English is reflected in their actual linguistic usage. The usage of these variables is investigated across gender and age groups to identify any evidence of change over time and gendered patterns. Furthermore, the study employs a language ideological framework which enables a locally meaningful account of the identified patterns of variation.
- Docherty, Gerard J. and Paul Foulkes (1999), 'Newcastle upon Tyne and Derby: instrumental phonetics and variationist studies', in Paul Foulkes and Gerard J. Docherty (eds), *Urban Voices: Accent Studies in the British Isles*, London: Arnold, pp. 47–71.
  This chapter provides an overview of the phonology of Tyneside English and an account of variation in the consonant system.
- Jones, Mark J. and Carmen Llamas (2008), 'Fricated realisations of /t/ in Dublin and Middlesbrough English: an acoustic analysis of plosive frication and surface fricative contrasts', *English Language and Linguistics*, 12.3: 419–43.
  This paper looks specifically at realisations of voiceless stops in Middlesbrough and undertakes a fine-grained acoustic analysis of the fricated forms of /t/. A comparison is made between such forms and realisations found in Dublin English.
- Kerswill, Paul E. (1984), 'Social and linguistic aspects of Durham (e:)', *Cambridge Papers in Phonetics and Experimental Linguistics*, vol. 2, 1983, Cambridge: University of Cambridge, Department of Linguistics.

This study analyses the social distribution of variants of the FACE variable in Durham in the 1980s in order to identify evidence of change in the use of its local and supra-local realisations.

- Llamas, Carmen (2001), 'The sociolinguistic profiling of (r) in Middlesbrough English', in Hans Van de Velde and Roeland van Hout (eds), *'r-atics: Sociolinguistic, Phonetic and Phonological Characteristics of /r/*, special issue of *Études et Travaux*, 4 December 2001, Brussels: ILVP, pp. 123–40.
  This paper deals specifically with age- and gender-correlated variation in the realisations of (r). The distribution of variants reveals both the levelling out of localised forms and the diffusion of innovatory forms into the variety.

- Llamas, Carmen (2006), 'Shifting identities and orientations in a border town', in Tope Omoniyi and Goodith White (eds), *Sociolinguistics of Identity*, London: Continuum, pp. 92–112.
  This chapter considers the shifting regional identity of Middlesbrough due to changing political boundaries and considers phonological variation and the change it implies in light of the changes to informants' shifting orientations.

- Llamas, Carmen (2007), 'A place between places: language and identities in a border town', *Language in Society*, 36.4: 579–604.
  This paper considers age- and gender-correlated variation in the realisations of voiceless stops in Middlesbrough English. How patterns of convergence and divergence relate to informants' attitudes towards their regional identities is explored.

- Maguire, Warren (2007), 'What is a merger, and can it be reversed? The origin, status and reversal of the "NURSE-NORTH Merger" in Tyneside English', PhD thesis, Newcastle University.
  This doctoral dissertation deals with the variation and change in the realisation of the NURSE vowel and the NORTH vowel in Tyneside English.

- Pearce, Michael (2009), 'A perceptual dialect map of North East England', *Journal of English Linguistics*, 37.2: 162–92.
  This paper reports the findings of a perceptual dialectology study in the North-East which aimed to explore North-Easterners' mental maps of language variation in their own region. Having identified three main dialect areas in the region (northern, central and southern), Pearce then goes on to explore whether there is any link between speakers' perception of variation and actual production.

- Watt, Dominic (2000), 'Phonetic parallels between the close-mid vowels of Tyneside English: are they internally or externally motivated?', *Language Variation and Change*, 12: 69–101.
  This paper looks at the levelling in lockstep of the FACE vowel and the

GOAT vowel in Tyneside English. Results are considered in relation to chain shift phenomena.

- Watt, Dominic (2002), '"I don't speak with a Geordie accent, I speak, like, the Northern accent": contact-induced levelling in the Tyneside vowel system', *Journal of Sociolinguistics*, 6.1: 44–63. *In this paper, Watt gives an account of variation and change in the vowel system of Tyneside English and argues that younger Tyneside speakers are converging on a levelled supraregional norm.*

5.3 Morphosyntax

- Beal, Joan C. (1993), 'The grammar of Tyneside and Northumbrian English', in James Milroy and Lesley Milroy (eds), *Real English: The Grammar of English Dialects in the British Isles*, London: Longman, pp. 187–213.
  This chapter was the first account of the distinctive features of morphology and syntax in Tyneside English. This is a descriptive account, based on sources available at the time. As such, it needs to be read in conjunction with more recent corpus-based studies of individual features, but still provides a good overview.
- Beal, Joan C. and Karen P. Corrigan (2002), 'Relativisation in Tyneside and Northumbrian English', in Pat Poussa (ed.), *Relativisation on the North Sea Littoral*, LINCOM Studies in Language Typology 7, Munich: Lincom Europa, pp. 125–34.
  This chapter provides an account of a small-scale study of variation and change in the use of relative markers in Tyneside English, based on data from the NECTE corpus.
- Beal, Joan C. and Karen P. Corrigan (2005a), 'A tale of two dialects: relativisation in Newcastle and Sheffield', in Markku Filppula, Marjatta Palander, Juhani Klemola and Esa Penttilä (eds), *Dialects Across Borders*, Amsterdam: Benjamins, pp. 211–29.
  This chapter provides a more nuanced account than Beal and Corrigan (2002), distinguishing between relative markers in subject and object position with animate and inanimate antecedents. It also provides a contrastive study with data from a corpus of a different northern variety of English.
- Beal, Joan C. and Karen P. Corrigan (2005b), '"No, nay, never": negation in Tyneside English', in Yoko Iyeiri (ed.), *Aspects of Negation in English*, Amsterdam: Benjamins, pp. 139–56.
  This chapter provides a corpus-based account of variation and change

in the negation system of Tyneside English, using data from the NECTE corpus.

- Buchstaller, Isabelle and Karen P. Corrigan (2011), 'How to make intuitions succeed: testing methods for analysing syntactic microvariation', in Warren Maguire and April McMahon (eds), *Analysing Variation in English*, Cambridge: Cambridge University Press, pp. 30–48.
  This chapter contains a detailed discussion of the theoretical and practical issues involved in collecting and analysing data on syntactic variation, together with examples drawn from the authors' research into Tyneside English.
- Snell, Julia (2010), 'From sociolinguistic variation to socially strategic stylization', *Journal of Sociolinguistics*, 14.5: 630–56.
  This paper reports on a quantitative sociolinguistic analysis of the first-person possessive singular pronoun in Teesside English. Data are collected from schoolchildren and usage is considered in relation to the speakers' stylised interactional performances.

5.4 Lexis

- Barnfield, Kate and Isabelle Buchstaller (2010), 'Intensifiers on Tyneside: longitudinal developments and new trends', *English World-Wide*, 31.3: 252–87.
  This paper presents a corpus-based account of variation and change in the use of intensifiers by Tyneside speakers. Using data from the new DECTE corpus, the authors are able to identify both patterns of recurrence and new trends.
- Burbano-Elizondo, Lourdes (2001), 'Lexical erosion and lexical innovation in Tyne and Wear', MLitt dissertation, Newcastle University.
  In this study Burbano-Elizondo investigated the extent to which traditional dialect words previously attested in the North-East by traditional studies (especially the SED) were still used or known by Sunderland and Newcastle adolescents at the beginning of the twenty-first century, and, if some of these had fallen out of use or were only part of the passive lexical repertoire of the speakers, this study aimed to ascertain what lexical items had replaced those that had undergone attrition among the young generation.
- Burbano-Elizondo, Lourdes (2006), 'Regional variation and identity in Sunderland', in Tope Omoniyi and Goodith White (eds), *The Sociolinguistics of Identity*, London: Continuum, pp. 113–28.

This chapter investigates the Sunderland identity and how community members define their community and perceive it as being linguistically different from other North-Eastern varieties.

- Simmelbauer, Andrea (2000), *The Dialect of Northumberland: A Lexical Investigation,* Heidelberg: Universitätsverlag C. Winter.
  This is an account of an investigation of lexical retention and loss based on a questionnaire-based study of speakers from Tyneside and Northumberland.

5.5 References cited in this text

Allen, Will, Joan C. Beal, Karen P. Corrigan, Warren Maguire and Hermann L. Moisl (2006), 'A linguistic "time capsule": the Newcastle Electronic Corpus of Tyneside English', in Joan C. Beal, Karen Corrigan and Hermann L. Moisl (eds), *Creating and Digitizing Language Corpora,* vol. 2: *Diachronic Databases,* Basingstoke: Palgrave Macmillan, pp. 16–48.

Anderwald, Liselotte (2002), *Negation in Non-standard British English,* London: Routledge.

Asprey, Esther (2007), 'Black Country English and Black Country identity', PhD thesis, University of Leeds.

Atkinson, John (2011), 'Linguistic variation and change in a North-East border town: a sociolinguistic study of Darlington', PhD thesis, Newcastle University.

Barnfield, Kate and Isabelle Buchstaller (2010), 'Intensifiers on Tyneside: longitudinal developments and new trends', *English World-Wide,* 31.3: 252–87.

Baugh, Arthur C. and Thomas Cable (1993), *A History of the English Language,* 4th edition, London: Routledge.

Beal, Joan C. (1985), 'Lengthening of *a* in Tyneside English', in Roger Eaton, Olga Fischer, Willem F. Koopman and Frederike van der Leek (eds), *Papers from the Fourth International Conference on English Historical Linguistics,* 10–13 April, Amsterdam, pp. 31–44.

Beal, Joan C. (1993), 'The grammar of Tyneside and Northumbrian English', in James Milroy and Lesley Milroy (eds), *Real English: The Grammar of English Dialects in the British Isles,* London: Longman, pp. 187–213.

Beal, Joan C. (1999), *English Pronunciation in the Eighteenth Century: Thomas Spence's 'Grand Repository of the English Language',* Oxford: Clarendon Press.

Beal, Joan C. (2000), 'From Geordie Ridley to *Viz:* popular literature in Tyneside English', *Language and Literature,* 9.4: 343–59.

Beal, Joan C. (2004), 'The phonology of English dialects in the north of England', in Bernd Kortmann (ed.), *A Handbook of Varieties of English,* Berlin: Mouton de Gruyter, vol. 1, pp. 113–33.

Beal, Joan C. (2008), 'English dialects in the north of England: morphology and syntax', in Bernd Kortmann and Clive Upton (eds), *Varieties of English I: The British Isles,* Berlin: Mouton de Gruyter, pp. 373–403.

Beal, Joan C. (2010), *An Introduction to Regional Englishes: Dialect Variation in England*, Edinburgh: Edinburgh University Press.

Beal, Joan C. and Lourdes Burbano-Elizondo (2010), '"All the lads and lasses": lexical variation in Tyne and Wear', paper presented at *Sociolinguistics Symposium 18 (SS18)*, 1–4 September, University of Southampton.

Beal, Joan C. and Karen P. Corrigan (2000), 'Comparing the present with the past to predict the future for Tyneside English', *Newcastle and Durham Working Papers in Linguistics*, vol. 6, pp. 13–30.

Beal, Joan C. and Karen P. Corrigan (2002), 'Relativisation in Tyneside and Northumbrian English', in Pat Poussa (ed.), *Relativisation on the North Sea Littoral*, LINCOM Studies in Language Typology 7, Munich: Lincom Europa, pp. 125–34.

Beal, Joan C. and Karen P. Corrigan (2005a), 'A tale of two dialects: relativisation in Newcastle and Sheffield', in Markku Filppula, Marjatta Palander, Juhani Klemola and Esa Penttilä (eds), *Dialects Across Borders*, Amsterdam: Benjamins, pp. 211–29.

Beal, Joan C. and Karen P. Corrigan (2005b), '"No, nay, never": negation in Tyneside English', in Yoko Iyeiri (ed.), *Aspects of Negation in English*, Amsterdam: Benjamins, pp. 139–56.

Beal, Joan C. and Karen P. Corrigan (2011), 'Inferring syntactic variation and change from the *Newcastle Electronic Corpus of Tyneside English* (NECTE) and the *Corpus of Sheffield Usage* (CSU)', VARIENG Studies in Variation, Contacts and Change in English 7. http://www.helsinki.fi/varieng/journal/volumes/07/beal_corrigan.

Briggs, Asa (1996), 'Middlesbrough: the growth of a new community', in A. J. Pollard (ed.), *Middlesbrough Town and Community, 1830–1950*, Stroud: Sutton Publishing, pp. 1–31.

Brockett, John T. (1825), *A Glossary of North County Words in Use*, Newcastle upon Tyne: Hodgson.

Buchstaller, Isabelle and Karen P. Corrigan (2011), 'How to make intuitions succeed: testing methods for analysing syntactic microvariation', in Warren Maguire and April McMahon (eds), *Analysing Variation in English*, Cambridge: Cambridge University Press, pp. 30–48.

Burbano-Elizondo, Lourdes (2001), 'Lexical erosion and lexical innovation in Tyne and Wear', MLitt dissertation, Newcastle University.

Burbano-Elizondo, Lourdes (2006), 'Regional variation and identity in Sunderland', in Tope Omoniyi and Goodith White (eds), *The Sociolinguistics of Identity*, London: Continuum, pp. 113–28.

Burbano-Elizondo, Lourdes (2008), 'Language variation and identity in Sunderland', PhD thesis, University of Sheffield.

Chase, Malcolm (1995), 'The Teesside Irish in the nineteenth century', *Cleveland History: The Bulletin of the Cleveland and Teesside Local History Society*, 69: 3–23.

Cheshire, Jenny, Viv Edwards and Pamela Whittle (1993), 'Non-standard English and dialect levelling', in James Milroy and Lesley Milroy (eds), *Real*

English: The Grammar of English Dialects in the British Isles, London: Longman, pp. 53–96.

Colls, Robert (1998), 'Cookson, Chaplin, Common: three northern writers in 1951', in K. D. M. Snell (ed.), *The Regional Novel in Britain and Ireland, 1800–1900*, Cambridge: Cambridge University Press, pp. 164–200.

Coombes, Mike (2005), *Tyne and Wear City Region: Emerging Polynuclearity* [final report], Centre for Urban and Regional Development Studies (CURDS), Newcastle University. Available at: http://www.thenorthernway.co.uk/downloaddoc.asp?id=24 (last accessed 6 October 2011).

Coupland, Nikolas (1992), *Dialect in Use*, Clevedon: Multilingual Matters.

Coupland, Nikolas and Hywel Bishop (2007), 'Ideologised values for British accents', *Journal of Sociolinguistics*, 11.1: 74–93.

Cruttenden, Alan (1997), *Intonation*, 2nd edition, New York: Cambridge University Press.

Defoe, Daniel (1753), *A Tour Thro' the Whole Island of Great Britain*, 5th edition, London: S. Birt, etc.

Denison, David (1998), 'Syntax', in Suzanne Romaine (ed.), *The Cambridge History of the English Language*, vol. IV: *1776–1997*, Cambridge: Cambridge University Press, pp. 92–326.

Docherty, Gerard J. and Paul Foulkes (1999), 'Newcastle upon Tyne and Derby: instrumental phonetics and variationist studies', in Paul Foulkes and Gerard J. Docherty (eds), *Urban Voices: Accent Studies in the British Isles*, London: Arnold, pp. 47–71.

Docherty, Gerard J., Paul Foulkes, James Milroy, Lesley Milroy and David Walshaw (1997), 'Descriptive adequacy in phonology: a variationist perspective', *Journal of Linguistics*, 33: 275–310.

Dodds, Glen L. (2001), *A History of Sunderland*, 2nd edition, Sunderland: Albion Press.

Ellis, Stanley (1994), 'The Yorkshire Ripper enquiry: Part 1', *Forensic Linguistics*, 1.2: 197–206.

Ellis, Joyce (2001), 'The "Black Indies": economic development of Newcastle, *c.* 1700–1840', in Robert Colls and Bill Lancaster (eds), *Newcastle upon Tyne: A Modern History*, Chichester: L. Phillimore, pp. 1–26.

Fiennes, Celia (1947), *The Journeys of Celia Fiennes*, ed. C. Morris, London: Cresset Press.

Finnegan, Katie (2011), 'Phonological variation and local identity in Sheffield', PhD thesis, University of Sheffield.

Foulkes, Paul (1997), 'English[r] sandhi- a sociolinguistic perspective', *Histoire Épistémologie Langage*, 19.1: 73–96.

Foulkes, Paul and Gerard J. Docherty (2000), 'Another chapter in the story of /r/: "labiodental" variants in British English', *Journal of Sociolinguistics*, 4.1: 30–59.

Foulkes, Paul, Gerard J. Docherty and Dominic Watt (1999), 'Tracking the emergence of sociophonetic variation in 2 to 4 year olds', *Leeds Working Papers in Linguistics and Phonetics*, vol. 7, pp. 1–25.

Foulkes, Paul, Gerard J. Docherty and Dominic Watt (2005), 'Phonological variation in child-directed speech', *Language*, 81.1: 177–206.

Gimson, Alfred C. (1989), *An Introduction to the Pronunciation of English*, 4th edn, revised by Susan Ramsaran, London: Edward Arnold.

Glauser, Beat (1985), 'BOYS AND GIRLS, SONS AND DAUGHTERS: the evidence of the *Survey of English Dialects* (SED)', *English World-Wide*, 6.1: 37–57.

Grabe, Esther, Brechtje Post, Francis Nolan and Kimberley Farrar (2000), 'Pitch accent realization in four varieties of British English', *Journal of Phonetics*, 28: 161–85.

Grabe, Esther, Greg Kochanski and John Coleman (2005), 'The intonation of native accent varieties in the British Isles: potential for miscommunication?', in K. Dziubalska-Kolaczyk and Joanna Przedlacka (eds), *English Pronunciation Models: A Changing Scene*, Linguistic Insights series 21, Oxford: Peter Lang.

Green, Adrian and A. J. Pollard (eds) (2007), *Regional Identities in North-East England, 1300–2000*, Woodbridge: Boydell.

Harris, John and Jonathan Kaye (1990), 'A tale of two cities: London glottaling and New York City tapping', *Linguistic Review*, 7: 251–74.

Hermeston, Rod (2011), '"The Blaydon Races": lads and lasses, song tradition, and the evolution of an anthem', *Language and Literature*, 20.4:269–8.

Heslop, Richard Oliver (1892), *Northumberland Words: A Glossary of Words Used in the County of Northumberland and on the Tyneside*, English Dialect Society 66, 68, 71, London: Kegan Paul.

Hickey, Raymond (2007), *Irish English: History and Present-Day Forms*, Cambridge: Cambridge University Press.

House, John W. (1969), *The North-East*, Newton Abbot: David and Charles.

Hughes, Arthur and Peter Trudgill (1979), *English Accents and Dialects*, London: Arnold.

Hughes, Arthur, Peter Trudgill and Dominic Watt (2005), *English Accents and Dialects*, 4th edition, London: Arnold.

Ihalainen, Ossi (1994), 'The dialects of England since 1776', in Robert Burchfield (ed.), *The Cambridge History of the English Language,* vol. V: *English Language in Britain and Overseas: Origins and Developments*, Cambridge: Cambridge University Press, pp. 197–274.

Institute for Name-Studies (2010), *Key to English Place-Names*. Available at: http://www.nottingham.ac.uk/~aezins//kepn.php (last accessed October 2011).

Jones, Mark (2002), 'The origin of definite article reduction in northern English dialects: evidence from dialect allomorphy', *English Language and Linguistics*, 6: 325–45.

Jones, Mark and Carmen Llamas (2003), 'Fricated pre-aspirated /t/ in Middlesbrough English', in Maria J. Solé, Daniel Recasens and Joaquin Romero (eds), *Proceedings of the 15th International Congress of Phonetic Sciences*, 3–9 August, Barcelona: Causal, pp. 655–8.

Jones, Mark and Carmen Llamas (2008), 'Fricated realisations of /t/ in Dublin and Middlesbrough English: an acoustic analysis of plosive frication and surface fricative contrasts', *English Language and Linguistics*, 12.3: 419–43.

Kerswill, Paul (1984), 'Social and linguistic aspects of Durham (e u)', *Journal of the International Phonetic Association*, 14: 13–34.

Kerswill, Paul (1987), 'Levels of linguistic variation in Durham', *Journal of Linguistics*, 23: 25–49.

Kerswill, Paul (2003), 'Dialect levelling and geographical diffusion in British English', in David Britain and Jenny Cheshire (eds), *Social Dialectology: In Honour of Peter Trudgill*, Amsterdam: Benjamins, pp. 223–43.

Kerswill, Paul and Ann Williams (2000), 'Creating a new town koine: children and language change in Milton Keynes', *Language in Society*, 29: 65–115.

Kerswill, Paul and Ann Williams (2002), 'Dialect recognition and speech community focusing in new and old towns in England: the effects of dialect levelling, demography and social networks', in Daniel Long and Dennis Preston (eds), *A Handbook of Perceptual Dialectology*, Amsterdam: Benjamins, vol. 2, pp. 178–207.

Kortmann, Bernd (2008), 'Synopsis: morphological and syntactic variation in the British Isles', in Bernd Kortmann and Clive Upton (eds), *Varieties of English I: The British Isles*, Berlin: Mouton de Gruyter, pp. 478–96.

Kortmann, Bernd and Benedikt Szmrecsanyi (2004), 'Global synopsis: morphological and syntactic variation in English', in Bernd Kortmann, Kate Burridge, Rajend Mesthrie, Edgar W. Schneider and Clive Upton (eds), *A Handbook of Varieties of English*, vol. 2: *Morphology and Syntax*, Berlin: Mouton de Gruyter, pp. 1142–202.

Lendrum, Oliver (2001), 'An integrated elite: Newcastle's economic development, 1840–1914', in Robert Colls and Bill Lancaster (eds), *Newcastle upon Tyne: A Modern History*, Chichester: L. Phillimore, pp. 27–46.

Llamas, Carmen (1999), 'A new methodology: data elicitation for social and regional language variation studies', *Leeds Working Papers in Linguistics and Phonetics*, vol. 7, pp. 95–118.

Llamas, Carmen (2001a), 'Language variation and innovation in Teesside English', PhD thesis, University of Leeds.

Llamas, Carmen (2001b), 'The sociolinguistic profiling of (r) in Middlesbrough English', in Hans Van de Velde and Roeland van Hout (eds), *'r-atics: Sociolinguistic, Phonetic and Phonological Characteristics of /r/*, special issue of *Études et Travaux*, 4 December 2001, Brussels: ILVP, pp. 123–40.

Llamas, Carmen (2006), 'Shifting identities and orientations in a border town', in Tope Omoniyi and Goodith White (eds), *The Sociolinguistics of Identity*, London: Continuum, pp. 92–112.

Llamas, Carmen (2007), '"A place between places": language and identities in a border town', *Language in Society*, 36: 579–604.

Llamas, Carmen, Peter French and Lisa Roberts (2010), 'Phonological and perceptual isoglosses between the Tyne and the Wear', paper presented at *Northern Englishes Workshop*, Sheffield, March 2010.

Local, John (1986), 'Patterns and problems in a study of Tyneside intonation', in Catherine Johns-Lewis (ed.), *Intonation and Discourse*, London: Croom Helm, pp. 181–98.

Local, John K., John Kelly and William H. G. Wells (1986), 'Towards a phonology of conversation: turn-taking in Tyneside English', *Journal of Linguistics*, 22: 411–37.

Macaulay, Ronald K. S. (2006), Pure grammaticalization: the development of a teenage intensifier', *Language Variation and Change*, 18.3: 267–83.

McDonald, Christine (1981), 'Variation in the use of modal verbs, with special reference to Tyneside English', PhD thesis, Newcastle University.

McDonald, Christine and Joan C. Beal (1987), 'Modal verbs in Tyneside English', *Journal of the Atlantic Provinces Linguistics Association*, 9: 42–55.

Maguire, Warren (2007), 'What is a merger, and can it be reversed? The origin, status and reversal of the "NURSE-NORTH merger" in Tyneside English', PhD thesis, Newcastle University.

Mair, Christian (2006), *Twentieth-Century English: History, Variation and Standardization*, Cambridge: Cambridge University Press.

Matras, Yaron (2007), 'Romani', *BBC Voices – Multilingual Nation*. Available at: http://www.bbc.co.uk/voices/multilingual/romani.shtml (last accessed October 2011).

Milroy, James (1995), 'Investigating the Scottish vowel length rule in a Northumbrian dialect', *Newcastle and Durham Working Papers in Linguistics*, vol. 4, pp. 187–96.

Milroy, James, Lesley Milroy and Sue Hartley (1994), 'Local and supra-local change in British English: the case of glottalisation', *English World-Wide*, 15.1: 1–33.

Milroy, James, Lesley Milroy, Sue Hartley and David Walshaw (1994), 'Glottal stops and Tyneside glottalisation: competing changes in British English', *Language Variation and Change*, 6: 327–57.

Milroy, Lesley (1987), *Observing and Analysing Natural Language: A Critical Account of Sociolinguistic Method*, Oxford: Blackwell.

Milroy, Lesley (1997), 'Gender, social class and supra-local norms: dialect levelling as language change', paper presented at *SALSA V: 1997*, Symposium about Language and Society – Austin, 13 April, University of Texas at Austin.

Milroy, Lesley (2002), 'Introduction: mobility, contact and language change – working with contemporary speech communities', *Journal of Sociolinguistics*, 6: 3–15.

Moisl, Hermann L. and Warren Maguire (2008), 'Identifying the main determinants of phonetic variation in the Newcastle Electronic Corpus of Tyneside English', *Journal of Quantitative Linguistics*, 15: 46–69.

Moisl, Hermann L., Warren Maguire and Will Allen (2006), 'Phonetic variation in Tyneside: exploratory multivariate analysis of the Newcastle Electronic Corpus of Tyneside English', in Frans Hinskens (ed.), *Language Variation – European Perspectives. Selected Papers from the Third International Conference on*

Language Variation in Europe (ICLaVE 3), Amsterdam, June 2005, Amsterdam: Benjamins, pp. 127–41.

Montgomery, Chris (2006), 'Northern English dialects: a perceptual approach', PhD thesis, University of Sheffield.

Moore, Emma and Julia Snell (2011), '"Oh, they're top, them": right dislocated tags and interactional stance', in Frans Gregersen, Jeffrey Parrott and Pia Quist (eds), *Language Variation – European Perspectives III. Selected Papers from the Fifth International Conference on Language Variation in Europe (ICLaVE 5), Copenhagen, June 2009*, Amsterdam: Benjamins, pp. 97–110.

Moorsom, Norman (1996), *Middlesbrough Re-Born: The Evolution of a Local Authority*, Middlesbrough: Moorsom.

Newcastle Electronic Corpus of Tyneside English. Available at: http://research.ncl.ac.uk/necte/ (last accessed October 2011).

NewcastleGateshead. Available at: http://www.newcastlegateshead.com/site/about-the-area/newcastlegateshead (last accessed October 2011).

O'Connor, Joseph D. (1973), *Phonetics*, London: Penguin.

OECD (Organisation for Economic Co-operation and Development) (2006), *Territorial Review: Newcastle in the North East, United Kingdom*, Paris: OECD Publishing.

Orton, Harold and Eugen Dieth (1962–71), *Survey of English Dialects*, Leeds: Arnold.

Orton, Harold and Natalia Wright (1974), *A Word Geography of England*, London: Seminar Press.

Orton, Harold, Stuart Sanderson and John D. A. Widdowson (1978), *The Linguistic Atlas of England*, London: Croom Helm.

Oxford English Dictionary. Available at: http://www.oed.com (last accessed February 2011).

Pandeli, Helen, Joseph F. Eska, Martin J. Ball and Joan Rahilly (1997), 'Problems of phonetic transcription: the case of the Hiberno-English slit-t', *Journal of the International Phonetic Association*, 27: 65–75.

Pearce, Michael (2009), 'A perceptual dialect map of North East England', *Journal of English Linguistics*, 37.2: 162–92.

Pearson, Harry (1994), *The Far Corner*, London: Waverley.

Pellowe, John, Graham Nixon, Barbara M. H. Strang, and Vincent McNeany (1972), 'A dynamic modelling of linguistic variation: the urban (Tyneside) Linguistic Survey', *Lingua*, 30: 1–30.

Pichler, Heike (2008), 'A qualitative-quantitative study of negative auxiliaries in a northern English dialect: I DON'T KNOW and I DON'T THINK, innit?', PhD thesis, University of Aberdeen.

Roach, Peter J. (1973), 'Glottalization of English /p/, /t/, /k/ and /tʃ/—a re-examination', *Journal of the International Phonetic Association*, 3: 10–21.

Romaine, Suzanne (1982), *Socio-Historical Linguistics: Its Status and Methodology*, Cambridge: Cambridge University Press.

Rowe, Charley (2007), '"He divn't gan tiv a college ti di that, man!" A study of do (and to) in Tyneside English', *Language Sciences* 29: 360–71.

Sankoff, David (1988), 'Sociolinguistics and syntactic variation', in Frederik J. Newmeyer (ed.), *Linguistics: The Cambridge Survey*, vol. IV: *Language: The Sociocultural Context*, Cambridge: Cambridge University Press, pp. 140–61.

Scobbie, James M., Nigel Hewlett and Alice E. Turk (1999), 'Standard English in Edinburgh and Glasgow: the Scottish vowel length rule revealed', in Paul Foulkes and Gerard J. Docherty (eds), *Urban Voices: Accent Studies in the British Isles*, London: Arnold, pp. 230–45.

Simmelbauer, Andrea (2000), *The Dialect of Northumberland: A Lexical Investigation*, Heidelberg: Universitätsverlag C. Winter.

Snell, Julia (2007), 'Give us my shoe back: the pragmatic functions of singular "us"', *Leeds Working Papers in Linguistics and Phonetics*, vol. 12, pp. 44–60.

Snell, Julia (2010), 'From sociolinguistic variation to socially strategic stylisation', *Journal of Sociolinguistics*, 14.5: 630–56.

Tagliamonte, Sali and Jennifer Smith (2002), '"Either it isn't or it's not": NEG/ AUX contraction in British dialects', *English World-Wide*, 23.2: 251–81.

Tees Valley Statistics (2010). Available at: http://www.teesvalleyunlimited. gov.uk/information-forecasting/documents/people_statistics/statistics%20 2010.pdf (last accessed October 2011).

Townsend, A. R. and Taylor, C. C. (1975), 'Regional culture and identity in industrialised societies: the case of North-East England', *Regional Studies*, 9: 379–93.

Trudgill, Peter (1986), *Dialects in Contact*, Oxford: Blackwell.

Trudgill, Peter (1990), *The Dialects of England*, Oxford: Blackwell.

Tulloch, Jonathan (2000), *The Season Ticket*, London: Jonathan Cape.

Upton, Clive S. and John D. A. Widdowson (1996), *An Atlas of English Dialects*, Oxford: Oxford University Press.

Upton, Clive S. and John D. A. Widdowson (1999), *Lexical Erosion in English Dialects*, Sheffield: National Centre for English Cultural Tradition.

Upton, Clive S., S. S. Sanderson and John D. A. Widowson (1987), *Word Maps: A Dialect Atlas of England*, London: Croom Helm.

Upton, Clive S., David Parry and John D. A. Widdowson (1994), *Survey of English Dialects: The Dictionary and Grammar*, London: Routledge.

Vall, Natasha (2001), 'The emergence of the post-industrial economy in Newcastle, 1914–2000', in Robert Colls and Bill Lancaster (eds), *Newcastle upon Tyne: A Modern History*, Chichester: L. Phillimore, pp. 47–70.

Vall, Natasha (2007), 'Regional and cultural history: the case of North-Eastern England, 1918–1976', in Adrian Green and A. J. Pollard (eds), *Regional Identities in North-East England, 1300–200*, Woodbridge: Boydell, pp. 181–208.

Viereck, Wolfgang (1966), *Phonematische Analyse des Dialekts von Gateshead-upon-Tyne/Co. Durham*, Hamburg: Cram, De Gruyter.

Viereck, Wolfgang (1968), 'A diachronic-structural analysis of a northern English vowel system', in Stanley Ellis (ed.), *Studies in Honour of Harold Orton on the Occasion of his 70th Birthday*, Leeds: University of Leeds School of English, pp. 65–79.

Wakelin, Martyn F. (ed.) (1972), *Patterns in the Folk Speech of the British Isles*, London: Athlone Press.

Wakelin, Martyn F. (1977), *English Dialects: An Introduction*, London: Athlone.

Wallace, Kate E. (2007), 'Social variation in the English of the Southampton area', PhD thesis, University of Leeds.

Wales, K. (2006), *Northern English: A Social and Cultural History*, Cambridge: Cambridge University Press.

Watson, Kevin (2007), 'Liverpool English', *Journal of the International Phonetics Association*, 37.3: 351–60.

Watt, Dominic (2000), 'Phonetic parallels between the close-mid vowels of Tyneside English: are they internally or externally motivated?', *Language Variation and Change*, 12: 69–101.

Watt, Dominic (2002), '"I don't speak with a Geordie accent, I speak, like, the Northern accent": contact-induced levelling in the Tyneside vowel system', *Journal of Sociolinguistics*, 6.1: 44–63.

Watt, Dominic and Will Allen (2003), 'Illustrations of the IPA: Tyneside English', *Journal of the International Phonetic Association*, 33.2: 267–71.

Watt, Dominic and Carmen Llamas (2004), 'Variation in the Middlesbrough English vowel system', poster presentation at the *British Association of Academic Phoneticians Colloquium*, Cambridge.

Watt, Dominic and Lesley Milroy (1999), 'Variation in three Tyneside vowels: is this dialect levelling?', in Paul Foulkes and Gerard J. Docherty (eds), *Urban Voices: Accent Studies in the British Isles*, London: Arnold, pp. 25–46.

Wells, John C. (1982), *Accents of English*, Cambridge: Cambridge University Press.

West, Helen (2009), '"I'm not Geordie! I'm not actually anything!" Convergent and divergent trends: dialect levelling and the struggle for identity in a south Durham new-town', MSc dissertation, University of Edinburgh.

Wright, Joseph (1892), *A Grammar of Windhill in the West Riding of Yorkshire*, London: Kegan Paul.

Wright, Joseph (1896–1905), *The English Dialect Dictionary*, London: Henry Frowde.

Index